Like Attracts Like

Thoughts Are Things

*Whatever Your Mind Can
Conceive and Believe,
You Can Achieve*

The Secret
Law of Attraction
as explained by
Napoleon Hill

The Secret

Law of Attraction

as explained by

Napoleon Hill

Edited by Bill Hartley and Ann Hartley
with commentary by Bill Hartley

HIGHROADS MEDIA, INC.

ISBN-10: 1-932429-37-9
ISBN-13: 978-1-932429-37-4
10 9 8 7 6 5 4 3 2 1

Contents

Publisher's Preface

As this book goes to press in 2008, it marks the centennial of one of the most important meetings in the history of publishing. It is the one-hundredth anniversary of the famous interview between Napoleon Hill and Andrew Carnegie that launched the best-selling success book ever written.

It was during this meeting that Carnegie first explained to Hill his personal interpretation of the Law of Attraction. It was also at this meeting that Carnegie challenged Hill to undertake what Carnegie predicted would be the twenty-year task of researching and writing a philosophy of success that could be used by the common man.

Andrew Carnegie's estimate was correct, and the result of Napoleon Hill's labors was first published in 1928 in the eight-volume masterwork, *Law of Success.* In 1937 Hill released a revised and refined version of his research, which became the classic motivational bestseller, *Think and Grow Rich.* Although both cover a wide range of business-related topics, at the heart of each book is what Hill referred to as the Carnegie secret, or the Law of Attraction.

For the first time, the editors of this book have carefully analyzed the original 1928 edition of *Law of Success* and the 1937 edition of *Think and Grow Rich* to identify those passages that focus on the Law of Attraction. We have excerpted the key sections from each book and brought them together in the following pages to reveal the secret of the Carnegie secret: the Law of Attraction, as explained by Napoleon Hill.

As the excerpts were being assembled into chapters, the editors approached the written text as we would that of a living author. When we encountered what modern grammarians would consider run-on sentences, outdated punctuation, or other matters of form, we opted for contemporary usage.

There is an editorial note that appears either before or after each excerpt identifying the original source material. You will notice that in some of the excerpts from *Law of Success,* Napoleon Hill uses the term "lesson" to refer to the material. The explanation is that when Hill was compiling this first book, he considered it to be a course of study, and each chapter in the book is actually called a lesson.

Some editing has been done to bring related sections of text into closer proximity to one another, but in every case the original context has been preserved and the original meaning remains unchanged. In a few instances, alterations have been made to correct scientific information that has since become outdated.

All editorial commentary is clearly set off in this sans serif font, which is different from the serif font used for the original text excerpted from either *Law of Success* or *Think and Grow Rich.*

About the Editors

For more than twenty years, the publisher/editors of this book, Bill Hartley and Ann Hartley, have not only been deeply involved in the study of Hill's writings, but have also been the leading publishers of his works. As publishers, producers, and editors, they have created and published more bestselling books and audiobooks by and about Napoleon Hill than any other publisher in the world.

Chapter I

The Carnegie Secret

&

The Law of Attraction

There are few events in recent times that have had as great an impact on popular culture as did the release of the documentary-style video program *The Secret*. Created by Australian television producer Rhonda Byrnes, featuring dramatizations reminiscent of the movie *The Da Vinci Code* and interspersed with commentary by contemporary motivational experts and authors, the program proclaims that from ancient times down through the ages the great minds of every era have jealously guarded the secret of transforming wishes into reality.

The Secret not only alludes to famous historical figures who possessed this arcane knowledge, but it also names a number of influential personages of the modern world who are said to have learned the secret of the Law of Attraction and used it to achieve positions of great importance, power, and wealth.

This book, *The Secret Law of Attraction as explained by Napoleon Hill,* focuses its attention on two of the more famous names mentioned as keepers of the secret—Andrew Carnegie and Napoleon Hill—and on how Carnegie conveyed his understanding of this secret Law of Attraction to Hill—who, in turn, transformed those concepts into the best-selling success book in the history of publishing: *Think and Grow Rich.*

NAPOLEON HILL, ANDREW CARNEGIE, AND THE NEW THOUGHT MOVEMENT

As a young man determined to make a name for himself in the world of business, it was only natural that Napoleon Hill would have read about the Law of Attraction in the popular books of the day associated with the New Thought Movement. This concept became more than just a passing interest on the day in the fall of 1908 when Hill was ushered through the door of the magnificent 64-room mansion at the corner of Fifth Avenue and 91st Street in New York City. He was awe-struck by the opulence that surrounded him as he stood in the grand foyer of Andrew Carnegie's Georgian manse, waiting for the butler to escort him to the library where he was to meet with the famed steel tycoon and philanthropist.

Napoleon Hill had been hired by a magazine to write a profile on Andrew Carnegie, and Hill had been granted three hours in which to interview him. However, by the end of the allotted time, Carnegie had become so taken with the intelligence of this intense young man that he kept extending their meeting, until the interview that had started on Friday finally came to an end the following Monday. Hill's entire career as an author is the result of what he learned from Andrew Carnegie at that meeting.

During their three-day marathon, Andrew Carnegie set forth in detail his personal philosophy of wealth and success. It was a philosophy that drew upon some of the ideas championed by the New Thought Movement—particularly the concept of the Law of Attraction—but Carnegie's version was tempered with the practical lessons learned by a man who had raised himself out of poverty to create one of the greatest fortunes the world has ever known.

ANDREW CARNEGIE

Andrew Carnegie was born in Scotland and was thirteen when he emigrated to America with his parents in 1848. He took his first step onto the ladder of success by quitting his job as a bobbin boy in a cotton mill, earning $1.20 a week, and getting a job as a Western Union telegraph messenger boy. That move put him in a position where he could teach himself to operate a telegraph key, which led to him being hired as personal telegrapher and secretary to the head of the Pennsylvania Railroad. From there he worked his way up through the ranks until he achieved the position of superintendent of the Pittsburgh division. A great believer in the role that railroads would play in America's future, Carnegie was an early investor in the Pullman company, which became the leading manufacturer of railway cars. It was Carnegie's investment in Pullman, plus some successful real estate ventures, that provided him the capital to go into business for himself.

In 1865, as the civil war was coming to an end, Carnegie tendered his resignation to the Pennsylvania Railroad in order to start his own company that would go into the business of building iron bridges for the railroads. From building iron bridges it was a short step to the manufacturing of rails, then locomotives, which led him to acquire control of his own iron and steel mills, then his own coal fields to supply his smelters, then his own ore boats and his own rail lines to haul the ore and coal. Because of the vertical integration of Carnegie's various companies, and because he insisted on using the most up-to-date and efficient manufacturing methods, he was able to sell top-grade steel at a lower price than his competitors. By 1899 he managed to drop the price of steel from $140 a ton to $20 a ton, and the Carnegie Steel Company then controlled about 25 percent of the iron and steel production in America.

In 1901 Andrew Carnegie was persuaded to sell his company to J.P. Morgan for $400 million (which would be comparable to approximately $8 billion at the beginning of the twenty-first century). It was Carnegie's company that Morgan used as the lynchpin in the creation of a new company that became the industrial giant U.S. Steel.

From the 1870s until his death in 1919, Andrew Carnegie strove to match his outstanding business success with his even greater philanthropic largesse. He built public libraries, endowed colleges, provided funding for schools and churches, and created numerous foundations, trusts, and institutions for the advancement of human rights, world peace, ethics, conflict prevention, and all levels of education, science, and the arts.

By almost every measure, Andrew Carnegie was one of the most successful men in the world.

NAPOLEON HILL

In 1883 Napoleon Hill was born in a two-room log cabin in the Appalachian Mountains of southwest Virginia in what he described as conditions of poverty, ignorance, and superstition: "For three generations my people had been born, lived, struggled, and died without ever having been outside the mountains of that section. There were no railroads, telephones, electric lights, or passable public highways." And there was little reason to think that anyone in the Hill clan would turn out any different.

His mother died when Napoleon Hill was barely nine years old, and with no mother to look after the family and with little parental supervision, young Nap turned into the local hell-raiser. Always stubborn and hot-tempered, he began carrying a six-gun stuffed into his belt, and most of the locals expected he would follow in the footsteps of the man he proclaimed as his hero: Jesse James.

Later in life, when Hill became famous as a public speaker, he often opened his speeches by telling his audience that theoretically he should not have been there with them. Rather, he should have been with his mountain-folk kin, carrying on feuds, killing rattlesnakes, and drinking "corn likker." But that all changed when Nap's father remarried and brought his new wife to live in their backwoods cabin.

Martha Ramey Banner was well-educated, cultured, the daughter of a physician, and the widow of a school principal, and she was little prepared for hillbilly living or a pistol-toting stepson. Something was going to change, and it wasn't going to be Martha. She vowed that she would not live in poverty, and from that moment on, the Hill clan was going to change its ways.

Within days of her arrival, Martha called her new family together and, one by one, she began planting the ideas that would inspire each of them to believe they could become more than what they were. Napoleon's father, James, who had been a poor dirt farmer and part-time blacksmith, became Wise County's most successful dentist. Napoleon's brother Vivian, who started his education in the local one-room school house, graduated from Georgetown University and joined a prestigious law practice in Washington, D.C., and Napoleon's stepbrother Paul followed a similar path to become a highly respected surgeon.

But it was in her most rebellious stepson that Martha saw the greatest promise. By the time Napoleon was twelve, Martha had convinced him to give her his pistol in exchange for a typewriter. She told him, "If you become as good with a typewriter as you are with that gun, you may become rich and famous and known throughout the world."

Her faith and encouragement turned young Nap's life around, and by the age of fifteen he was submitting stories to the local newspapers and doing everything he could to get himself out of his meager circumstance. After graduation he went away to a one-year business school, then convinced a local mine operator to hire him, and by the age of nineteen he was the youngest manager of a coal mine, supervising 350 men.

After three years in the Virginia mining industry, Napoleon Hill moved to Washington, D.C., where he studied law at Georgetown for a year, then became a partner in a lumber business until the bank failure of 1907 decimated his business. This prompted him to turn to his typewriter once again as a way to make a living.

Napoleon Hill knew of Robert L.Taylor as the past governor of Hill's home state of Virginia, who had become the publisher of *Bob Taylor's Magazine,* a Washington-based publication that specialized in inspirational stories for those striving to get ahead in business. Writing for such a magazine seemed to Hill like something he would be perfect at.

Robert Taylor had heard of Napoleon Hill as a bright young man who'd made quite a name for himself back home in Virginia. That intrigued Taylor enough to meet with the self-declared journalist, and he found that he not only liked him, but he also liked Hill's proposal to write a series of success profiles. His first choice was to interview Andrew Carnegie, and that's how Napoleon Hill managed to secure that fateful first meeting.

THE NEW THOUGHT MOVEMENT

Coinciding with Hill's formative years and with Carnegie's rise to wealth and success, a philosophical trend called the New Thought Movement —based on the power of positive thinking—was gaining influence in

America. Phineas Quimby, generally acknowledged as the father of the movement, was a healer and a practitioner of hypnosis who came to believe that the healing he was able to effect was not caused by him, but rather it was being done by the power of the patient's own mind.

Quimby's theory that the power of thought can produce change in the real world was not original to him, but because his sphere of friends and associates included a number of influential people, his ideas began to have a significant impact. New Thought began to emerge as a movement around 1850, and reached its zenith from the turn of the century through the 1930s.

One of Quimby's patients, author Warren Felt Evans, was so impressed by the way he was cured that he wrote a number of books about "mental science" and its application in healing. Learning of the technique, William James, the father of American psychology, wrote and lectured on what he called "the mind cure."

Another of Quimby's patients, Mary Baker Eddy, adapted belief in the power of the mind as the basis of the Christian Science Church and, in turn, her associate Emma Curtis Hopkins went on to teach the philosophy to Myrtle and Charles Filmore, who founded the Unity Church. Hopkins also taught Ernest Holmes, who founded the Church of Religious Science.

Although the early offshoots of Quimby's work were primarily concerned with using the power of the mind to effect healing in the body, others in the movement focused on the Law of Attraction's ability to create not only health but also wealth and success.

Often expressed by the phrase "like attracts like," this concept proposes that positive thoughts held in the mind attract positive results in reality. The emphasis on self-improvement brought to the movement writers such as Ralph Waldo Trine who wrote *Character Building—Thought Power.* Charles Haanel wrote the still-in-print classic *The Master Key System.* William Watkins Atkinson wrote more than one hundred books on the subject, including *Thought Vibrations or the Law of Attraction in the Thought World.* Orison Scott Marden wrote fifty books, with such titles as *Every Man a King* and *Pushing to the Front.* Marden was also the creator and publisher of *Success Magazine* which, except for a brief hiatus, was still on the stands in 2008—one hundred and thirteen years after its first issue. Also influential in the New Thought Movement was Wallace Wattles, whose 1906 book *The Science of Getting Rich* would be credited a century later by Rhonda Byrnes as one of her major inspirations when she created her video program *The Secret.*

However, by far the most successful and enduring of all the books that speak to the power of the Law of Attraction is *Think and Grow Rich* by Napoleon Hill.

NAPOLEON HILL LEARNS THE CARNEGIE SECRET

For three days Napoleon Hill listened as Andrew Carnegie explained the secret of his extraordinary success. And it is significant that "the secret" was exactly the way Carnegie phrased it: singular, not plural. Although there were a number of factors that figured in Carnegie's success—and over three days and nights he covered an enormous range of subjects and explained a wide variety of ideas—to Carnegie they were all aspects of the one secret.

When Napoleon Hill published his first book based on what he had learned from Andrew Carnegie, Hill made certain that Carnegie's point of view was clear even in the title. Despite the fact that the book details sixteen separate principles, it was intentionally titled *Law of Success*. Singular, not plural.

Later, when Hill wrote his classic, *Think and Grow Rich,* the first sentence he wrote was about the Carnegie secret:

In every chapter of this book, mention is made of the money-making secret that has made fortunes for the exceedingly wealthy men whom I have carefully analyzed over a long period of years.

The secret was first brought to my attention by Andrew Carnegie. The canny, lovable old Scotsman carelessly tossed it into my mind when I was but a boy. Then he sat back in his chair, with a merry twinkle in his eyes, and watched carefully to see if I had brains enough to understand the full significance of what he had said to me.

Fortunately, Napoleon Hill did have the brains to understand the significance of what Carnegie was saying, and before the weekend was over he would have the chance to prove it.

It was Mr. Carnegie's idea that the magic formula, which gave him a stupendous fortune, ought to be placed within reach of people who do not have the time to investigate how others had made their money. It was his hope that I might test and demonstrate the soundness of the formula through the experience of men and women in every calling.

At the time of their meeting it had been seven years since Andrew Carnegie had sold his business holdings and devoted himself to public service and his many philanthropic pursuits. In Napoleon Hill he saw the possibility to advance one of these pursuits. To quote from *A Lifetime of Riches,* Napoleon Hill's biography, Carnegie told Hill:

My early days of youth were cursed with poverty and limited opportunity; a fact with which all who know me are acquainted. I am no longer cursed by poverty because I took possession of my mind, and that mind has yielded me every material thing I want, and much more than I need. But this power of the mind is a universal one, available to the humblest person as it is to the greatest.

It's a shame that each new generation must find the way to success by trial and error, when the principles are really clear-cut.

Carnegie went on to explain that one of his greatest passions was to guide the development of a comprehensive, written philosophy of success that could be understood and used by the average person. He told Hill he believed that to do it properly would require a series of lengthy, in-depth interviews with hundreds of the most successful leaders in every walk of life, as well as extensive research, testing, and analysis that could take as much as twenty years to complete. Then, in his famously blunt fashion, Carnegie turned to Hill and asked if Hill felt that he was equal to the task.

Surprised to be put on the spot but still caught up in Carnegie's lofty vision, Napoleon Hill's answer was an unreserved *yes*. This was an answer that displayed a self-confidence which would be sorely tested a minute or two later when it became clear that Carnegie was not offering to pay Hill to work on the project.

Carnegie explained that his own contribution to the creation of this philosophy would be to introduce Hill to the most successful and influential men in the world so Hill could learn directly from them the secret of their success. Carnegie made it clear that he would make the introductions and cover the necessary travel expenses, but Hill's reward would not be a salary. Rather, it would be in the doors that would be opened to him, in the special knowledge that he would become privy to, and finally, in the satisfaction and accolades he would receive for bringing to the world the first philosophy of individual achievement.

Though Napoleon Hill wasn't quite sure how he would manage it, he reaffirmed his commitment to take on the project and see it through to the end. Shortly thereafter, Andrew Carnegie began to arrange for Hill to meet with and study the most successful and powerful people of the day.

Hill was granted unprecedented access to interview and thoroughly investigate the business practices, personal influences, and private lives of the most successful businessmen, industrialists, inventors, scientists, authors, artists, and leaders of every kind.

Andrew Carnegie wanted Napoleon Hill to prove to himself that the secret he had explained to him was not just some eccentric millionaire's harebrained idea. He wanted Hill to convince himself that even though each of these famous and successful men had their own ways of doing things, the secret that helped them rise to the top was the same secret that Carnegie had revealed to Hill during their three-day meeting.

And that was how Napoleon Hill became the central figure in the process of analyzing the Carnegie secret in order to devise a practical method for the average person to use in creating their own success.

Although Andrew Carnegie died in 1919, the seed he had planted continued to bear fruit, as the leaders of business and industry whom Hill had met through Carnegie in turn introduced Hill to other equally important figures who also agreed to explain to him the secret of their success.

Throughout all the years of research, Napoleon Hill supported himself, his family, and the cost of the Carnegie project by creating a number of business ventures. He became a sales trainer, an educator, served as an adviser to corporations and government agencies, he worked for politicians and presidents, he became an in-demand lecturer, a writer, and, perhaps most significantly, he became a magazine publisher.

HE WROTE THOUSANDS OF WORDS EVERY MONTH

Between 1918 and 1924, Hill launched and published two monthly magazines: *Hill's Golden Rule* and *Napoleon Hill's Magazine.* It was the need to fill the pages of his magazines that prompted Hill to begin committing to paper the principles behind the secret of success he learned from Carnegie's famous friends, and to turn his own personal triumphs and failures into lessons. In these magazine articles Hill honed his theories, refined his arguments, and polished his presentation of the success philosophy for the common man that Andrew Carnegie had envisioned.

Hill published his first book based on the Carnegie secret in 1928. It was called *Law of Success* and it was the culmination of his twenty years of research into the habits of more than one hundred of the most successful individuals in America, as well as more than 16,000 interviews with average working people, business managers, and entrepreneurs. It was published as eight separate but interconnected volumes. No one had ever seen anything like it before. It was a phenomenon, a masterwork in eight parts, and it was a runaway bestseller.

Nine years later, in 1937, after having worked with many of the next generation's most influential people including a stint as a presidential adviser in FDR's White House, Napoleon Hill updated and reorganized his research. By this time the total number of interviews conducted by Hill had grown to 25,000 individuals. More than 500 of those were personal, in-depth interviews with the wealthiest and most influential entrepreneurs and leaders who were instrumental in America's rise to greatness.

The resulting book, *Think and Grow Rich,* is the best-selling success book ever published.

THIS BOOK FOCUSES ON JUST THE CARNEGIE SECRET

The task Andrew Carnegie had set for Napoleon Hill was for him to take the Carnegie secret of success, compare and contrast it with what he would learn from other people of great accomplishment, and then turn his findings into a written philosophy of success.

Because there was such a kaleidoscope of differing professions and personalities, as Hill investigated how each one came to learn the secret of success, he found that he was also being exposed to techniques of management, motivation, leadership, and other contributing factors which obviously should be included in a book that hoped to present a complete philosophy of success.

As a consequence, Hill's books not only explain the Carnegie secret but they also offer advice on everything from theoretical concepts such as decision-making and methods for increasing creativity, to nuts-and-bolts issues like budgeting time and money.

This book, *The Secret Law of Attraction as explained by Napoleon Hill,* has a much more focused objective. It sets aside Hill's other material in order to concentrate exclusively on the secret Law of Attraction. For the first time, the editors of this book have systematically gone through each chapter of *Law of Success* and *Think and Grow Rich* to separate those passages that deal with the Carnegie secret from those that deal with other concepts. The key sections were then excerpted from the original sources and brought together in this new book in a way that presents a clear and concise view of *The Secret Law of Attraction as explained by Napoleon Hill.*

When Hill wrote *Think and Grow Rich,* in the author's preface he pointed out that readers will recognize the Carnegie secret at least once in every chapter and that it is mentioned no fewer than one hundred times throughout the book. In the introduction he says this:

> When the famed English poet William Henley wrote the prophetic lines "I am the master of my fate, I am the captain of my soul," he should have informed us that the reason we are the masters of our fate, the captains of our souls, is that we have the power to control our thoughts.
>
> He should have told us that it is because in some way our brains become "magnetized" with the dominating thoughts that we hold in our minds. And it is as though our magnetized minds attract to us the forces, the people, and the circumstances of life that are in sync with our dominating thoughts.

Here is how Napoleon Hill wrote about it in *Law of Success,* in the lesson titled A Definite Chief Aim:

> The subconscious mind may be likened to a magnet; when it has been vitalized and thoroughly saturated

with any definite purpose, it has a decided tendency to attract all that is necessary for the fulfillment of that purpose.

Like attracts like, and you may see evidence of this law in every blade of grass and every tree. The acorn attracts from the soil and the air the necessary materials out of which to grow an oak tree. It never grows a tree that is part oak and part poplar. Every grain of wheat that is planted in the soil attracts the materials out of which to grow a stalk of wheat. It never makes a mistake and grows both oats and wheat on the same stalk.

LIKE ATTRACTS LIKE

The phrase "like attracts like" and the explanation that the mind is like a magnet, both of which appear in the preceding excerpts from Hill's books, are found throughout New Thought literature as a kind of shorthand for the law of attraction. In essence it means that what you focus on and hold in your mind will draw unto itself thoughts and ideas of a similar nature. Another phrase common among New Thought writers—"thoughts are things"—takes it a step further, conveying the idea that not only will the *thoughts* you think attract similar thoughts to your mind, but the *things* you think about will attract similar things which will come to you as *real* things in the real world.

In short, the Law of Attraction states that whatever you focus on in your mind acts like a magnet, attracting other like-natured ideas and concepts. If the thought you focus on is of a specific thing, that thought will manifest itself as the physical embodiment of the thought, and that thought will have become a thing.

Detractors say the idea that thoughts can alter reality, by attracting to you the things you think about, suggests that the universe is like some great mail-order catalog in the sky that will deliver all the goodies you wish for if you just think the right thoughts. They say that at the very least this kind of something-for-nothing thinking creates unrealistic expectations in those naïve enough to believe it, and at its worst it cruelly holds out false hope to those who are desperate for real help.

Could this be true? Was Andrew Carnegie really so naïve? Did Napoleon Hill really get taken in for thirty years?

Not likely.

In their effort to belittle the Law of Attraction, its critics portray it as far more simplistic than the way in which it was interpreted by Andrew Carnegie. Clearly the man who knew more than anyone else of his generation about the achievement of success and the creation of wealth was not proposing that all you have to do is think about something and it will suddenly deposit itself in your bank account or park itself in your driveway.

There is a vast difference between the critics' implication that the Law of Attraction means that what you wish for will just materialize, and the concept that a thought can become manifest as a reality. The critics ignore a whole host of actions that might transpire between the time a thought is first conceived and the time when it is finally realized. It is the difference between wanting something so much that you are constantly daydreaming about how nice it would be to have it, and wanting something so much that you are constantly thinking about what you can do to make it happen. The following explanation by Napoleon Hill is adapted from *Law of Success*:

> Everyone wishes for the better things in life such as money, a good position, fame and recognition; but most people never go far beyond the wishing stage. Men who know exactly what they want of life and are determined to get it, do not stop with wishing. They intensify their wishes into a burning desire, and back that desire with continuous effort based on a sound plan.
>
> All riches and all material things that anyone acquires through self-effort begin in the form of a clear, concise mental picture of the thing one seeks. When that picture grows, or it has been forced to the proportions of an obsession, it is taken over by the subconscious mind. From that point on, one is drawn, attracted, or guided

in the direction of the physical equivalent of the mental picture.

Visualizing your desire can't put actual dollars in your bank or park a Rolls-Royce in your driveway any more than it can make a cup and saucer suddenly materialize on the desk in front of you. When you visualize yourself acquiring money, a car, or any other real object, what you are really doing is confirming to yourself the belief that you are capable of making it happen. The vivid images that you create of your desire are burned into your subconscious, where they connect and interact with other bits of information, so that you automatically start coming up with more and better ideas of how you can earn the money to put in your bank so you can buy the Rolls-Royce.

Visualization doesn't create concrete objects; it creates attitudes and ideas. When you change your attitudes and ideas, you go from living inside your head to making things happen in the real world, and then it is *you*—not your visualization—who takes action and makes the concrete things come true.

Chapter 2

The Law of Attraction: How It Works & Why It Works

As Napoleon Hill pursued the research and interviews that would become the written explanation of the Carnegie secret, he came to the conclusion that the way the Law of Attraction works is actually the result of two separate functions—one he called Infinite Intelligence and the other he called Cosmic Habitforce. Infinite Intelligence accounts for *how* the Law of Attraction works, and Cosmic Habitforce explains *why* it works.

Although the format of this book is to present the Carnegie secret using excerpts from Hill's bestselling books, because it will make the content of the following chapters so much clearer if you understand these two concepts at the outset, the editors have assembled this short explanatory chapter.

Following is a step-by-step overview of the connections between Infinite Intelligence, Cosmic Habitforce, and the Law of Attraction.

- The Law of Attraction says that you are like a magnet that draws to yourself whatever you desire and focus on in your mind.

- The reason a thought or desire in your mind can attract to you the real object of your desire is that the thought and the reality share a connection with each other.

- The way a thought is connected with its reality is through Infinite Intelligence, which is Hill's term for the common link or connection between everything in the universe.

- What makes this common link or connection between all things is that every individual thing is some form of energy. Every object, every creature, and every force is just a different version of the same stuff: energy.

- Every individual thing also has a built-in propensity, a natural habit or way of being. Every creature, object, or force will follow its natural habit or instinct unless something steps in to change it.

- The human mind has its natural habit or propensity. It is the natural habit of the human mind to try to transform any thought or desire into the physical counterpart of that thought. That is what Hill calls the Cosmic Force of Habit (or Habitforce).

- Humans have the unique ability to consciously change their thoughts, so unlike every other thing that follows instinct, you can control what your mind focuses on, and therefore make Cosmic Habitforce work to your advantage.

To sum up: Because you can control what thought is in your mind, and because it is your mind's natural habit to try to make your thoughts come true, when you consciously plant a thought in your mind, it is automatic for your mind to try to make your thought come true through any means possible.

THE "HOW" AND "WHY" OF THE LAW OF ATTRACTION

The Law of Attraction is the name used to describe what Cosmic Habitforce and Infinite Intelligence do together.

Infinite Intelligence is *how* you get a response when you hold a thought in your mind.

Cosmic Force of Habit is *why* you get a response when you hold a thought in your mind.

The Law of Attraction states that any thought you hold in your mind will attract to you the physical counterpart of the thought, but it is Cosmic Habitforce that provides your mind with the method to do it, and it is Infinite Intelligence that provides the actual connections to send out the thought and receive the responses.

INFINITE INTELLIGENCE:
HOW THE LAW OF ATTRACTION WORKS

When you put the Law of Attraction to work it is like sending an SOS to the universe asking for answers. What Infinite Intelligence does is give you access to ideas that wouldn't normally occur to you, including hunches, gut feelings, and sudden flashes of insight.

Because intuition so often provides the kind of answers you need to make your life better, the following explains how you get these ideas and where they come from. We begin with this explanation excerpted and adapted from the opening chapter of *Law of Success*:

As far as science has been able to determine, the entire universe consists of but four things: time, space, matter, and energy. Moreover—and this statement is of stupendous importance—this earth, every one of the billions of individual cells of your body, and every subatomic particle of matter, began as an intangible form of energy. Through the combination of energy and matter has been created everything perceptible, from the largest star in the heavens down to and including man himself.

Desire is a thought impulse. Thought impulses are forms of energy. When you begin the process of acquiring money by using the thought impulse of desire, you are drafting into your service the same "stuff" that nature used in creating this earth, as well as every material form in the universe including your body and your brain in which the thought impulses function.

Napoleon Hill says everything from the stars to the solar system to the planet earth, to you, your brain, and that little spark called a thought are all comprised of the same "stuff."

To illustrate, imagine a tablecloth spread out before you. There are folds and bumps in the fabric that are all different from each other, but each fold or bump is still made up of the same tablecloth; like the folds and bumps in the tablecloth, energy and matter are made up of the same thing, just in different forms. Hill calls this interrelation of everything to everything else Infinite Intelligence.

INFINITE INTELLIGENCE AND YOUR SUBCONSCIOUS MIND

Infinite Intelligence is probably best thought of as a system, in the same way that you think of a broadcasting system or a telephone system. Your subconscious mind is what connects you into the system, and it does so in three ways: It is your "sending station" when you send out an idea of what you want to attract into your life. It is also your "receiving station" for ideas that come back to you from Infinite Intelligence. And it is your storehouse of bits and pieces of information and ideas from which new solutions are created.

YOUR SUBCONSCIOUS IS A STOREHOUSE OF IDEAS

Your conscious mind receives information through the five senses of touch, sight, hearing, taste, and smell, and your subconscious has access to all the same information, but your subconscious mind doesn't filter or judge information or ideas the way your conscious mind does. It just takes in all information and stores it.

Your subconscious doesn't make value judgments. It doesn't draw a distinction between good and bad, or positive and negative. Your subconscious takes everything literally—and it doesn't forget anything.

What your subconscious does respond to is the intensity with which an idea is planted. The stronger the emotion attached to an idea when planted in your subconscious, the more prominent that idea will be.

YOUR SUBCONSCIOUS IS YOUR "SENDING STATION"

Your subconscious mind is the "sending station" through which vibrations of thought are broadcast. Autosuggestion is the way in which you put your "sending station" into operation.

An autosuggestion is any suggestion you give to yourself. If you wish to change some aspect of yourself, you can do so by creating a self-suggestion that tells your "self" that you wish to make this change in the way you think or act.

By repeating your self-suggestion over and over in the form of positive affirmations or creative visualizations, your new desire will become embedded in your subconscious mind, which automatically makes it a part of the system of Infinite Intelligence.

YOUR SUBCONSCIOUS IS ALSO YOUR "RECEIVER"

You receive thoughts from your subconscious when information and ideas that are stored below the conscious level come together and flash into your creative imagination.

Most ideas that flash into your imagination are made up from bits of information and ideas that your conscious mind has filtered out or forgotten. Because your subconscious never forgets, those bits of information remain in your subconscious until your mind signals that it needs an idea, which stimulates the bits of information in your subconscious to create a new idea that flashes into your mind.

Sometimes other kinds of ideas that we call hunches or insights flash into your mind from your subconscious, but they are not made up from forgotten information. In fact, these ideas were not even received through any of your five senses. These are the ideas that come from Infinite Intelligence.

HOW YOU "RECEIVE" IDEAS FROM INFINITE INTELLIGENCE

- When humans think thoughts and create ideas, the activity in the mind-brain generates pulses of energy.

- The pulses of energy created by an idea send waves radiating outward from the thinker, similar to broadcasting radio waves radiating from an antenna.

- Like the radio waves that are part of the electromagnetic spectrum which is traveling around us and within us at all times, thought waves are part of the Infinite Intelligence that is also around us and within us at all times.

- The pulsating energy that is generated by your mind-brain is created at a particular frequency.

- If another thinker's idea is sending pulses of energy out through Infinite Intelligence at the same frequency that your mind-brain is attuned to, your mind-brain receives that idea from Infinite Intelligence.

- When your physical brain intercepts these waves, the ideas and information that the waves are carrying become a part of the store of ideas in your subconscious mind.

- At the subconscious level, all the bits of filtered and forgotten information and ideas are constantly interconnecting with each other and fitting together with ideas that were picked up through Infinite Intelligence to create new ideas and solutions that weren't there before.

Whether you call it a hunch, a gut feeling, instinct, suspicion, mother's intuition, premonition, empathy, first impression, instant dislike, or love at first sight, when information that entered your subconscious from Infinite Intelligence flashes into your mind, it feels unusual and you don't quite know why you thought of it. It doesn't feel like it is the logical result of what you know.

Hill says the reason you don't know "where on earth that idea came from" is simply that it's not your idea. It doesn't come from your own experience. It's a thought wave rippling through Infinite Intelligence, which happened to be of the right frequency to become part of your subconscious, and when your conscious mind focused on thoughts of a similar nature, it flashed into your imagination.

COSMIC FORCE OF HABIT:
WHY THE LAW OF ATTRACTION WORKS

The material in each chapter of this book is drawn from the relevant chapters in Hill's books, but the concept of the Cosmic Force of Habit didn't actually come to Hill until after *Think and Grow Rich* was already published. Following is how Hill describes it in one of his lectures:

There is something behind the lines of that book, there's a feeling you pick up as you read it. After *Think and Grow Rich* came out, I commenced to get telegrams and letters and telephone calls from all over the world congratulating me on account of this book. After this had gone on for about a month I said to myself, well by golly, I'm going to read that book. Maybe that fella's got something I don't know about.

Then I sat down to read my own book, and I just disassociated myself from it as though I had never seen it before, and about the middle of the book it came to me. The idea came to me that gave me the principle of cosmic habitforce.

I had been searching for that down through the years and hadn't found it until I read it in my own book. It wasn't something I had written and forgotten, it was something there between and behind the lines.

What Hill recognized as he reread what he had written was that the advice and lessons and stories in his book all added up to the idea that there is a force at work in the universe, and it is this force that makes the Carnegie secret work.

This was especially striking to Napoleon Hill because Andrew Carnegie had specifically cautioned him to focus on *how* to use his philosophy of success, and to avoid the question of *why* it worked. Carnegie's reasoning was that he wanted to be sure the philosophy could be used by people of all faiths.

When I first started out with Andrew Carnegie, he had admonished me to never under any circumstances attach any title of an orthodox nature to this philosophy. He said the minute you do that, you will split your audience.

Hill did as Carnegie advised and avoided any reference to God, but even so, the message people were taking from *Think and Grow Rich* is that there is some kind of force at work that turns thoughts into reality.

Hill realized that to avoid any misunderstanding he would have to be more explicit about *why* the Law of Attraction worked, and what this "force" had to do with it. First, the reason it works isn't just accident or coincidence, and it's not anything mystical or magical either. The force that is at work is what is commonly referred to as the force of habit.

All things in the universe have a habitual way of doing things. Every individual thing has its built-in propensity or instinct, and unless blocked for some reason, its inclination is to follow its natural habit.

The Law of Attraction works because it is the mind's natural habit that when it focuses on a thought, its automatic response is to try to make that thought into a reality. Thoughts become things.

Could it really be that simple?

COSMIC FORCE OF HABIT: A LAW OF NATURE

Although on first hearing it seems too simplistic, Hill's final answer to the question of *why* the Law of Attraction works is that it works because that is what the mind does. That is the mind's habit. It is only following the law of nature.

A law of nature is determined when a certain stimulus produces the same result time after time, until it is accepted that it is its nature to produce that result every time, all the time.

For thirty years Napoleon Hill had studied thousands of the most successful people and analyzed the relationship between what they believed and the success they achieved. The connection between the Law of Attraction and great success happened so consistently, it convinced him that the way in which the mind responded was no accident, but was in fact a predictable law of nature.

COSMIC FORCE OF HABIT AND FREE WILL

The following is adapted from Napoleon Hill's explanation excerpted from *Law of Success: The 21st-Century Edition*:

> Every living thing below the intelligence of man lives, reproduces itself, and fulfills its earthly mission in direct response to the power of the Cosmic Force of Habit through what we call *instinct*.

Man alone has been given the privilege of choice in connection with his living habits, and these he may fix by the patterns of his thoughts.

You may control your destiny to an astounding degree —simply by exercising the privilege of shaping your own thoughts. Once these thoughts have been shaped into definite patterns, they are taken over by the law of Cosmic Habitforce and are made into permanent habits, and they remain as such unless and until they have been supplanted by different and stronger thought patterns.

In all of nature there are fixed habits. Water always has two atoms of hydrogen, never one; apple seeds never grow into orange trees; and nobody ever falls off the earth for lack of gravity.

Every aspect of life relies upon the laws of nature to make sure that if we do A, then B will always be the result.

Cosmic Habitforce is the law of nature that says habits become part of your nature through repetition. If you keep repeating certain ideas in your mind, Cosmic Habitforce will take over those patterns of thought and make them your natural reaction.

It can work for you, or it can work against you.

Your mind will take whatever it is given and try to turn that into reality. If your mind is filled with the fear of failure, that is exactly what your mind will try to make happen.

But if you intentionally change your thinking and focus your mind on the anticipation of succeeding, your mind will work to give you success instead.

In both cases, no matter whether your mind was attracting failure or attracting success, Cosmic Habitforce was the reason why your mind transformed the thought into reality.

Chapter 3

Your Desire

or

Definite Chief Aim

The first principle that Napoleon Hill writes about in *Law of Success* is called A Definite Chief Aim, and in *Think and Grow Rich* the corresponding chapter is titled Desire. The central point in both is that to transform thoughts into reality, the first step is to have a clearly conceived idea of what it is that you wish to achieve.

Although the term "a definite chief aim" seems to imply something important and all-encompassing, what Hill actually meant is that anything you wish for, big or small, has a chief aim and that you must be definite and specific about what that aim is. Your desire or definite chief aim might be one specific goal, it could be a larger objective, or it may be the overarching philosophical precept that guides your whole life; if you wish to transform it from thought to reality you must know exactly how you want it to manifest itself.

The items that follow are excerpted from a number of chapters in both books, but all deal with the concept of your definite chief aim or desire. The first is adapted from *Law of Success*:

The psychological principles upon which this lesson is founded:

First, every voluntary movement of the human body is caused, controlled, and directed by thought, through the operation of the mind.

Second, the presence of any thought or idea in your consciousness tends to produce an associated feeling and urge you to transform that feeling into appropriate muscular action that is in perfect harmony with the nature of the thought.

Stating this principle from another angle: You choose, for example, a definite purpose and make up your mind that you will carry out that purpose. From the very moment that you make this choice, this purpose becomes the dominating thought in your consciousness, and you are constantly on the alert for facts, information, and knowledge with which to achieve that purpose. From the time that you plant a definite purpose in your mind, your mind begins, both consciously and unconsciously, to gather and store away the material with which you are to accomplish that purpose.

Desire is the factor that determines what your definite purpose in life shall be. No one can select your dominating desire for you, but once you select it yourself it becomes your definite chief aim and occupies the spotlight of your mind until it is transformed into reality, unless you permit it to be pushed aside by conflicting desires.

Until you select a definite chief aim in life you dissipate your energies and spread your thoughts over so many subjects and in so many different directions that they lead not to power but to indecision and weakness.

With the aid of a magnifying glass you can teach yourself a great lesson on the value of organized effort. Through the use of such a glass you can focus the sun's rays on a definite spot so strongly that they will burn a hole through a plank. Remove the glass (which represents the definite purpose) and the same rays of sun may shine on that same plank for a million years without burning it.

Napoleon Hill would often illustrate a point by using stories about the wealthy and powerful men he'd had the opportunity to meet and interview. It was through Thomas Edison that Hill got to know Edwin C. Barnes, whose story Hill liked to cite as a prime example of what the power of the mind can accomplish when it's focused on a clearly defined desire or chief aim.

Hill recounted the Barnes story in both *Law of Success* and *Think and Grow Rich,* and the following combines excerpts from both:

THE INVENTOR AND THE TRAMP

Truly, "thoughts are things." And powerful things, when they are mixed with definiteness of purpose, persistence, and a burning desire for their translation into riches, or other material objects.

Some years ago, Edwin C. Barnes discovered how true it is that you really can think and grow rich. His discovery did not come about at one sitting. It came little by little, beginning with a burning desire to become a business associate of the great Thomas Edison.

One of the chief characteristics of Barnes' desire was that it was definite. He wanted to work *with* Edison, not *for* him. Pay close attention to the story of how he turned his desire into reality, and you will have a better understanding of the principles that lead to riches.

When this desire, or this thought, first flashed into his mind he was in no position to act upon it. Two problems stood in his way. He did not know Mr. Edison, and he did not have enough money to buy a train ticket to West Orange, New Jersey, where the famed Edison laboratory was located.

These problems would have discouraged the majority of people from making any attempt to carry out the desire. But his was no ordinary desire! He was so determined to find a way to carry out his desire that he finally decided to travel by "blind baggage," rather than be defeated. (To the uninitiated, this means that he went to West Orange on a freight train.)

When Edwin C. Barnes climbed down from the freight train in West Orange, he may have resembled a tramp but his thoughts were those of a king.

As he made his way from the railroad tracks to Thomas A. Edison's office, his mind was at work. He saw himself standing in Edison's presence. He heard himself asking Mr. Edison for an opportunity to carry out the one consuming obsession of his life—a burning desire to become the business associate of the great inventor.

Barnes' desire was not a hope, and it was not a wish. It was a pulsating desire, which transcended everything else. It was a definite chief aim.

Edwin C. Barnes presented himself at Mr. Edison's laboratory, and when asked to state his business, before being permitted to see Mr. Edison, the young man boldly replied, "I am going to become his partner!"

His boldness got him past the secretary. An hour later he was at work, scrubbing floors in the Edison plant.

That hour of selling was worth millions of dollars. Five years later Barnes was a partner of the great Edison, he accumulated a fortune, and he owed every cent of it to the hour he spent in private conversation with Edison. During that hour he sold himself so thoroughly that it gave him his opportunity to go into partnership with one of the greatest men this country ever produced.

Years later, in speaking about that first meeting, Mr. Edison said about Barnes:

> He stood there before me, looking like an ordinary tramp, but there was something in the expression of his face which conveyed the impression that he was determined to get what he had come after. I had learned, from years of experience with men, that when a man really desires a thing so deeply that he is willing to stake his entire future on a single turn of the wheel in order to get it, he is sure to win. I gave him the opportunity he asked for, because I saw he had made up his mind to stand by until he succeeded. Subsequent events proved that no mistake was made.

Barnes did not get his partnership with Edison on his first interview. What he did get was a chance to work in the Edison offices, at a very nominal wage.

Months went by. Nothing happened to bring nearer the goal that Barnes had set as his definite major purpose. But something important was happening in Barnes' mind. He was constantly intensifying his desire to become the business associate of Edison.

Psychologists have correctly said, "When one is truly ready for a thing, it puts in its appearance." Barnes was ready for a business association with Edison. And he was determined to remain ready until he got what he was seeking.

He did not say to himself, "Ah well, what's the use? I guess I'll change my mind and try for a salesman's job." But he did say, "I came here to go into business with Edison, and I'll accomplish my goal if it takes the remainder of my life." He meant it. What a different story people would tell if only they would adopt a definite purpose and stand by that purpose until it had time to become an all-consuming obsession.

Maybe young Barnes did not know it at the time, but his bulldog determination, and his persistence in focusing on a single desire, was destined to mow down all opposition and bring him the opportunity he was seeking.

Five years passed before the chance he had been seeking made its appearance. To everyone, except himself, he appeared to be just another cog in the Edison business wheel. But in Edwin Barnes' own mind, he was the partner of Edison every minute from the very day that he first went to work there.

When the opportunity came, it appeared in a different form and from a different direction than Barnes had expected. That is one of the tricks of opportunity. It has a sly habit of slipping in by the back door. And often it comes disguised in the form of misfortune, or temporary defeat. Perhaps this is why so many people fail to recognize opportunity.

Mr. Edison had just perfected a new device, known at that time as the Edison Dictating Machine. His salesmen were not enthusiastic about the machine. They did not believe it could be sold without great effort. Barnes saw his opportunity. It had crawled in quietly, hidden in a queer-looking machine that interested no one but Barnes and the inventor.

Barnes knew he could sell the Edison Dictating Machine and he told Edison so. Edison decided to give him his chance. And Barnes did sell the machine. In fact, he sold it so successfully that Edison gave him a contract to distribute and market it all over the nation. Out of that business association Barnes made himself rich in money, but he did something greater. He proved that you really can think and grow rich.

How much actual cash that original desire of Barnes' was worth to him, I have no way of knowing. Perhaps it brought him two or three million dollars [three million dollars in the early years of the twentieth century would be comparable to more than sixty million dollars in terms of buying power at the beginning of the twenty-first century]. But the amount becomes insignificant compared with the greater asset he acquired: the definite knowledge that an intangible impulse of thought can be transmuted into material rewards by the application of known principles.

Barnes literally thought himself into a partnership with the great Edison! He thought himself into a fortune. He had nothing to start with, except knowing what he wanted, and the determination to stand by that desire until he realized it. He made himself the number-one man with the greatest inventor who ever lived.

It is a remarkable illustration of the power of a definite desire. Barnes won his goal because he wanted to be a business associate of Mr. Edison's more than he wanted anything else. He created a plan by which to attain that purpose, and he burned all bridges behind him. He stood by his desire until it became the dominating obsession of his life—and finally, a fact.

Edwin Barnes not only focused his mind on making his definite aim into a reality, he also focused on making a plan to make it come true. That is a distinction in Andrew Carnegie's interpretation of the Law of Attraction that Hill elaborates on in the following section, adapted from *Law of Success*:

It is a well-established principle of psychology that a person's acts are always in harmony with the dominating thoughts of his or her mind. The keynote of this entire lesson may be found in the word *definite*.

Any definite chief aim that is deliberately fixed in the mind and held there, with the firm determination to realize it, finally saturates the entire subconscious mind until it automatically influences the physical action of the body toward the attainment of that purpose.

Your definite chief aim should be selected with deliberate care, and after it has been selected it should be written out and placed where you will see it at least once a day. The psychological effect of this is to impress this purpose upon your subconscious mind so strongly that it accepts this purpose as a pattern or blueprint that will eventually dominate your activities in life and lead you, step by step, toward the attainment of the object behind that purpose.

The principle of psychology through which you can impress your definite chief aim on your subconscious mind is autosuggestion, or suggestion that you repeatedly make to yourself. It is a form of self-hypnotism, but do not be afraid of it, for it was through the aid of this same principle that Thomas Edison rose from his lowly beginning to become accepted as the leading inventor of the world. It was also through the aid of this principle that Abraham Lincoln bridged the mighty chasm between his lowly birth, in a log cabin in the mountains of Kentucky, and the presidency of the greatest nation on earth.

The following excerpt adds further clarification about the use of autosuggestion and the importance of taking action:

Science has established, beyond the slightest room for doubt, that through the principle of autosuggestion any deeply rooted desire saturates the entire body and mind with the nature of the desire and literally transforms the mind into a powerful magnet that will attract the object of the desire, if it is within reason.

For those who might not properly interpret the meaning of this statement, I will explain this principle in another way. For example, merely desiring an automobile will not cause that automobile to come rolling in. But if there is a *burning desire* for an automobile, that desire will lead to the appropriate action through which an automobile may be paid for.

The following section sets out specific steps to employ the Carnegie secret. It is excerpted and adapted from *Think and Grow Rich.*

SIX WAYS TO TURN DESIRE INTO GOLD

The method by which your desire for riches can be transmuted into its financial equivalent consists of six definite, practical steps:

1. Fix in your mind the exact amount of money you desire. It is not sufficient merely to say "I want plenty of money." Be definite about the amount. (There is a psychological reason for such definiteness explained in subsequent chapters.)

2. Determine exactly what you intend to give in return for the money you desire. (There is no such reality as "something for nothing.")

3. Establish a definite date by which you intend to possess the money you desire.

4. Create a definite plan for carrying out your desire and begin at once, whether you are ready or not, to put this plan into action.

5. Now write it out. Write a clear, concise statement of the amount of money you intend to acquire, name the time limit for its acquisition, state what you intend to give in return for the money, and describe clearly the plan through which you intend to accumulate it.

6. Read your written statement aloud, twice daily. Read it once just before retiring at night, and read it once after arising in the morning. As you read, see and feel and believe yourself already in possession of the money.

It is important that you follow the instructions in these six steps. It is especially important that you observe and follow the instructions in the sixth step. You may complain that it is impossible for you to "see yourself in possession of money" before you actually have it. Here is where a burning desire will come to your aid.

If you truly desire money so keenly that your desire is an obsession, you will have no difficulty in convincing yourself that you will acquire it. The object is to want money, and to become so determined to have it that you convince yourself you will have it.

The following two excerpts adapted from *Law of Success* make a perfect restatement of the basic premise of this chapter and the way to put it to work:

The object of your definite chief aim should become your hobby. You should ride this hobby continuously; you should sleep with it, eat with it, play with it, work with it, live with it, and *think* with it.

Whatever you want you may get—if you want it with sufficient intensity, and keep on wanting it, providing the object wanted is one within reason, and you actually believe you will get it!

There is a difference, however, between merely wishing for something and actually believing you will get it. A lack of understanding of this difference has meant failure to millions of people.

APPLYING THE PRINCIPLES OF THIS LESSON

It must have occurred to you that you might as well have no definite chief aim unless you also have a very definite and practical plan for turning that aim into a reality. Your first step is to decide what your major aim in life shall be. Your next step is to write out a clear, concise statement of that aim.

This should be followed by a statement, in writing, of the plan or plans through which you intend to attain the object of your aim.

You are now ready to begin using this principle as a means of transforming your definite chief aim into reality.

Chapter 4

Faith in Yourself
&
The Law of Habit

You have learned that any idea you firmly fix in your subconscious mind, by repeated affirmation, automatically becomes a plan or blueprint that an unseen power uses in directing your efforts toward the attainment of the objective named in the plan.

You have also learned that the principle through which you may fix in your mind any idea you choose is called autosuggestion, which simply means a suggestion that you give to your own mind.

Just as electricity will turn the wheels of industry and serve mankind in a million other ways, or snuff out life if wrongly applied, so will this principle of autosuggestion lead you up the mountainside of peace and prosperity, or down into the valley of misery and poverty, according to the application you make of it.

If you fill your mind with doubt and unbelief in your ability to achieve, then the principle of autosuggestion takes this spirit of unbelief and sets it up in your subconscious mind as your dominating thought, and slowly but surely it draws you into the whirlpool of *failure.*

But if you fill your mind with radiant self-confidence, the principle of autosuggestion takes this belief and sets it up as your dominating thought and helps you master the obstacles that fall in your way until you reach the mountaintop of success.

The preceding is excerpted from the chapter in *Law of Success* titled Self-Confidence. The section that follows draws upon excerpts adapted from the parallel chapter in *Think and Grow Rich,* which is titled Faith: Visualization of and Belief in Attainment of Desire.

In modern usage, the word *faith* has become interchangeable with "religious belief," which is not the way Hill uses the word. Faith, as it is used here, means having confidence, trust, and an absolute, unwavering belief that you can do something. And in order for you to have faith in yourself as Hill means it, it has to be true on a subconscious level. If you have a nagging doubt in the back of your mind, or if you are just going through the motions of pretending you believe, it won't work because your subconscious will know your doubts. Unless you have total confidence, unless you are convinced without question, then you don't have faith.

FAITH AND AFFIRMATIONS

The following statement is very important in understanding the importance of autosuggestion in the transmutation of desire into its physical or monetary equivalent; namely, faith is a state of mind that may be induced, or created, by affirmation or repeated instructions to the subconscious mind, through the principle of autosuggestion.

The repetition of affirmations is like giving orders to your subconscious mind, and it is the only known method of voluntary development of the emotion of faith (absolute belief that you can do something).

As an illustration, consider why you are reading this book —you want to acquire the ability to transmute the intangible thought impulse of desire into its physical counterpart: money. By following the instructions laid down in the later chapters on autosuggestion and the subconscious mind, you will learn techniques to convince your subconscious mind that you believe you will receive that for which you ask.

Your subconscious will act upon that belief, and pass it back to you in the form of "faith," followed by definite plans for procuring what you desire.

The emotions, or the "feeling" portion of thoughts, are what give your thoughts vitality, life, and action. All thoughts that have been emotionalized (given feeling) and mixed with faith (absolute belief in your ability) begin immediately to translate themselves into their physical equivalent or counterpart.

However, this is not only true of thought impulses that have been mixed with faith, but it is true with any emotion, including negative emotions.

What this means is that the subconscious mind will translate into its physical equivalent a thought impulse of a negative or destructive nature just as readily as it will act upon thought impulses of a positive or constructive nature.

This is the equivalent of saying that a negative impulse of thought that is repeatedly passed on to the subconscious mind often enough is, finally, accepted and acted upon by the subconscious mind. The subconscious then proceeds to translate that impulse into its physical equivalent, by the most practical procedure available.

This also accounts for the strange phenomenon that so many millions of people experience, referred to as bad luck.

There are millions of people who believe themselves doomed to poverty and failure because of some strange force they call bad luck, over which they believe they have no control. But the truth is that they are the creators of their own misfortunes, because this negative belief in bad luck is picked up by the subconscious mind and translated into its physical equivalent.

Your belief, or faith, is the element that will determine the action of your subconscious mind. Once again let me stress that you will benefit by passing on to your subconscious mind any desire that you wish translated into its physical or monetary equivalent, in a state of expectancy or belief that the transmutation will actually take place. The subconscious mind will transmute into its physical equivalent, by the most direct and practical way available, any order that is given to it in a state of belief or faith that the order will be carried out.

LIKE THOUGHTS ATTRACT LIKE THOUGHTS

It is a fact that you will come to believe whatever you repeat to yourself, whether the statement is true or false. If you repeat a lie over and over, you will eventually accept that lie as truth. Moreover, you will *believe* it to be the truth. You are what you are because of the dominating thoughts that you permit to occupy your mind. Thoughts that you deliberately place in your own mind, and encourage with sympathy, and with which you mix any one or more of the emotions, constitute the motivating forces that direct and control your every movement, act, and deed.

The following sentence is a very significant statement of truth: Thoughts that are mixed with any of the feelings of emotion become like a magnetic force, which attracts other similar or related thoughts.

A thought that is "magnetized" with one of the emotions may be compared to a seed. When it is planted in fertile soil, it germinates, grows, and multiplies itself over and over again. What was originally one small seed becomes countless millions of seeds of the same kind.

The human mind is constantly attracting vibrations that are in sync with whatever dominates the mind. Any thought, idea, plan, or purpose that you hold in your mind attracts a host of its relatives. Add these "relatives" to its own force, and it grows until it becomes the prime motivator of the person in whose mind it has been housed.

Now, let us go back to the starting point. How can the original seed of an idea, plan, or purpose be planted in the mind? The answer: Any idea, plan, or purpose may be placed in the mind through repetition of thought. This is why you are asked to write out a statement of your major purpose, or definite chief aim, commit it to memory, and repeat it out loud, day after day, until these vibrations of sound have reached your subconscious mind.

You are what you are because of the dominating thoughts that you permit to occupy your mind. If you choose to, you can throw off any bad influences from your past, and build your own life the way you want it to be. For instance, by taking inventory of your mental assets and liabilities, you might discover that your greatest weakness is lack of self-confidence. This can be overcome, and translated into courage, through the principle of autosuggestion. You can do this by writing out a set of simply stated, positive thought impulses, memorizing them, and repeating them until they become a part of the working equipment of your subconscious mind.

The following is an example for someone whose definite purpose is to overcome a lack of self-confidence.

Self-Confidence Formula

I. I know that I have the ability to achieve the object of my definite purpose in life. Therefore, I demand of myself persistent, continuous action toward its attainment, and I here and now promise to render such action.

2. I realize that the dominating thoughts of my mind will eventually reproduce themselves in outward, physical action, and will gradually transform themselves into physical reality. Therefore, I will concentrate my thoughts for thirty minutes each day, visualizing the person I intend to become. In this way I will create in my mind a clear mental picture.

3. I know, through the principle of autosuggestion, that any desire I persistently hold in my mind will eventually find some practical means of attaining my objective. Therefore, I will devote ten minutes daily to demanding of myself the development of self-confidence.

4. I have clearly written down a description of my definite chief aim in life, and I will never stop trying until I have developed sufficient self-confidence for its attainment.

5. I fully realize that no wealth or position can last unless it is built upon truth and justice. Therefore, I will engage in no transaction that does not benefit all whom it affects. I will succeed by attracting to myself the forces I wish to use, and the cooperation of other people. I will persuade others to help me, because of my own willingness to help others. I will eliminate hatred, envy, jealousy, selfishness, and cynicism, by developing love for all humanity, because

I know that a negative attitude toward others can never bring me success. I will cause others to believe in me, because I will believe in them and in myself.

6. I will sign my name to this formula, commit it to memory, and repeat it aloud once a day, with full faith that it will gradually influence my thoughts and actions so that I will become a self-reliant, and successful, person.

Behind this formula is the law of nature that psychologists call autosuggestion or self-suggestion. It is a proven technique that will work for your success, if it is used constructively. On the other hand, if used destructively, it will destroy just as readily. In this statement may be found a very significant truth; namely, that those who go down in defeat, and end their lives in poverty, misery, and distress, do so because of negative application of the principle of autosuggestion. All impulses of thought have a tendency to clothe themselves in their physical equivalent.

Thinking

If you *think* you are beaten, you are,
If you *think* you dare not, you don't;
If you like to win, but you *think* you can't,
It is almost certain you won't.

If you *think* you'll lose, you're lost,
For out in the world we find,
Success begins with a fellow's will—
It's all in the *state of mind.*

If you *think* you are outclassed, you are,
You've got to *think* high to rise;
You've got to be *sure of yourself* before
You can ever win a prize.

Life's battles don't always go
To the stronger or faster man,
But soon or late, the man who wins
Is the man who *thinks* he can!

—WALTER D. WINTLE

The following section is excerpted and adapted from the chapter titled Self-Confidence, which appears in *Law of Success*:

FAITH AND THE LAW OF HABIT

The object in writing out and repeating your definite aim or desire is to form the habit of making belief in yourself the dominating thought of your mind until that thought has been thoroughly embedded in your subconscious mind, through the principle of habit.

You first learned how to write by repeatedly directing the muscles of your arm and hand over certain letter outlines, until finally you formed the habit of tracing these outlines. Now you write quickly and easily, without tracing each letter slowly. Writing has become a *habit* with you.

The principle of habit will take hold of the faculties of your mind just the same as it will influence the physical muscles of your body, as you can easily prove by mastering and applying this lesson on self-confidence. Any statement that you repeatedly make to yourself, or any *desire* that you deeply plant in your mind through repeated statement, will eventually seek expression through your physical, outward bodily efforts. The principle of habit is the very foundation upon which this lesson on self-confidence is built.

The next section is excerpted and adapted from the chapter titled Concentration, which appears in *Law of Success*:

THE FORCE OF HABIT

It has been said that all people are the creatures of habit, and that habit is a cable; we weave a thread of it each day until it becomes so strong that we cannot break it.

If it is true that habit can compel you against your will, desire, and inclination, and thereby dominate your actions and character, then it can also be mastered, harnessed, and directed for your good. Thousands of people have applied this knowledge and have turned the force of habit into new channels.

A habit is a "mental path" over which your actions have traveled for some time, each passing making the path a little deeper and a little wider. If you have had to walk over a field or through a forest, you know how natural it is to choose the clearest path. The line of mental action is precisely the same. It is movement along the lines of least resistance—passage over the well-worn path.

Habits are created by repetition and formed in accordance to a natural law. The best way that old habits may be broken is to form new habits to counteract and replace the undesirable ones. Form new mental paths over which to travel, and soon the old ones will become less distinct. Every time you travel over the path of the desirable mental habit, you make that new path deeper and wider—and so much easier to travel thereafter.

This mental pathmaking is very important, and I cannot urge you too strongly to start making the desirable mental paths over which you wish to travel.

The following are the rules through which you may form the habits you desire:

I.   At the beginning of the formation of a new habit, put force and enthusiasm into your expression. Feel what you think. Remember that you are taking the first steps toward making your new mental paths, and it is much harder at first than it will be afterward. At the beginning, make each path as clear and as deep as you can, so that you can readily see it the next time you wish to follow it.

2.   Keep your attention firmly concentrated on your new path-building, and forget all about the old paths. Concern yourself only with the new ones that you are building to order.

3.   Travel over your newly made paths as often as possible. Create opportunities for doing so, without waiting for them to arise through luck or chance. The more often you go over the new paths, the sooner they will become well worn and easily traveled.

4.   Resist the temptation to travel over the older, easier paths you have been using in the past. Every time you resist a temptation, the stronger you become and the easier it will be for you to do so the next time. But every time you yield to the temptation, the easier it becomes to yield again and the more difficult it becomes to resist the next time. This

is the critical time. Prove your determination, persistency, and willpower now, at the very beginning.

5. Be sure you have mapped out the right path as your definite chief aim, then go ahead without fear and without allowing yourself to doubt. Select your goal and make good, deep, wide mental paths leading straight to it.

As you will have observed, there is a close relationship between habit and autosuggestion. Through habit, an act repeatedly performed in the same manner has a tendency to become permanent, and eventually we come to perform the act automatically or unconsciously. In playing a piano, for example, the artist can play a familiar piece while his or her conscious mind is on some other subject.

Autosuggestion is the tool with which we dig a mental path, concentration is the hand that holds that tool, and habit is the map or blueprint that the mental path follows. An idea or desire, to be transformed into terms of action or physical reality, must be held in the conscious mind faithfully and persistently until habit begins to give it permanent form.

We absorb the material for thought from our surrounding environment. The term *environment* covers a very broad field. It consists of the books we read, the people with whom we associate, the country and community in which we live, the nature of the work we do, the clothes we wear, the songs we sing, and, most important of all, the religious and intellectual training we receive prior to the age of fourteen.

The purpose of analyzing the subject of environment is to show its direct relationship to the personality you are developing, and how its influence will give you the materials out of which you may attain your definite chief aim in life.

The mind feeds upon that which you supply it, or that which is forced upon it, through your environment. Therefore, select your environment, as much as possible, with the object of supplying the mind with suitable material out of which to carry on its work. If your environment is not to your liking, change it!

The first step is to create in your own mind a clear, well-defined picture of the environment in which you believe you could best attain your definite chief aim. Then concentrate your mind on this picture until you transform it into reality.

Your daily associates constitute one of the most important and influential parts of your environment, and they may work for your progress or against it. As much as possible, you should select as your closest daily associates those who are in sympathy with your definite chief aim. You should make it a point to associate with people whose mental attitudes inspire you with enthusiasm, self-confidence, determination, and ambition.

Remember that every word spoken within your hearing, every sight that reaches your eyes, and every sense impression that you receive through any of the five senses, influences your thoughts. This being true, you can see the importance of controlling, as far as possible, the environment in which you live and work. You can see the importance of reading books which deal with subjects that are directly related to your definite chief aim. You can see the importance of talking with people who are in sympathy with your aims, and who will encourage you and spur you on toward their attainment.

The following section is adapted from the chapter titled The Habit of Saving, excerpted from *Law of Success*:

LIMITATION BUILT THROUGH HABIT

Millions of people go through life in poverty and want because they have made destructive use of the law of habit. Not understanding either the law of habit or the law of attraction through which "like attracts like," those who remain in poverty seldom realize that they are who they are and where they are as the result of their own acts.

Fix in your mind the thought that your ability is limited to a given earning capacity, and you will never earn more than that—the law of habit will set up a definite limitation of the amount you can earn. Your subconscious will accept this limitation, and very soon you will feel yourself "slipping" until finally you will become so hedged in by a fear of poverty that opportunity will no longer knock at your door; your doom will be sealed; your fate fixed.

Stating this great law in another way, when you thoroughly understand the law of habit, you may ensure yourself success in the great game of moneymaking by "playing both ends of that game against the middle."

You proceed in this manner:

First, through your definite chief aim, you set up in your own mind an accurate, definite description of what you want, including the amount of money you intend to earn. Then your subconscious mind takes over this picture you have created and uses it as a blueprint, chart, or map by which to mold your thoughts and actions into practical plans for attaining the object of your chief aim, or purpose. Through the law of habit you keep the object of your definite chief aim fixed in your mind until it becomes firmly and permanently implanted there.

This practice will destroy your poverty consciousness and it will set up in its place a prosperity consciousness. You will actually begin to demand prosperity, you will begin to expect it, you will begin to prepare yourself to receive it and to use it wisely.

Second, having in this manner increased your earning power, you will then make further use of the law of habit by saving a definite proportion of all the money you earn.

Therefore, as your earnings increase, your savings will likewise increase in proportion.

By demanding of yourself increased earning power, on the one hand, and by systematically laying aside a definite amount of all your earnings, on the other hand, you will soon reach the point at which you have removed all imaginary limitations from your own mind and you will then be well on the road toward financial independence.

Form the habit of thinking and talking of prosperity and abundance, and very soon material evidence will begin to manifest itself in the nature of wider opportunity, and new and unexpected opportunity.

Like attracts like! If you are in business and have formed the habit of talking and thinking about business being bad, business will be bad.

Fear of poverty is a negative, destructive state of mind. Moreover, one negative state of mind has a tendency to attract other similar states of mind. For example, the fear of poverty may attract the fear of ill health, and these two may attract the fear of old age, so that the victim finds themself poverty-stricken, in ill health, and actually growing old long before the time they should begin to show signs of old age.

Chapter 5

Enthusiasm, Self-Control, & Persistence

More than twenty years ago I became enthusiastic over an idea. When the idea first took form in my mind, I was unprepared to take even the first step toward its transformation into reality. But as I nursed it in my mind, I became enthusiastic as I looked ahead, in my imagination, and saw the time when I would be prepared to make it a reality.

The idea was this: I wanted to become the editor of a magazine, based on the Golden Rule, through which I could inspire people to keep up courage and deal with one another squarely.

Finally my chance came, and on Armistice Day 1918, I wrote the first editorial for what was to become the material realization of a hope that had lain dormant in my mind for nearly twenty years.

With enthusiasm I poured into that editorial the emotions which I had been developing in my heart. My dream had come true—my editorship of a national magazine had become a reality.

As I said, this editorial was written with enthusiasm. I took it to a man of my acquaintance, and with enthusiasm I read it to him. The editorial ended with these words: "At last my twenty-year-old dream is about to come true. It takes money, and a lot of it, to publish a national magazine, and I haven't the slightest idea where I am going to get this essential factor, but this is worrying me not at all because I know I am going to get it somewhere!" As I wrote those lines, I mixed enthusiasm and faith with them.

I had hardly finished reading this editorial when the man to whom I read it—the first and only person to whom I had shown it—said:

"I can tell you where you are going to get the money, for I am going to supply it." And he did!

Yes, enthusiasm is a vital force; so vital, that no one who has it highly developed can begin to even approximate their power of achievement.

Before moving to the next step in this lesson, I wish to repeat and to emphasize the fact that you may develop enthusiasm over your definite chief aim in life whether you are in position to achieve that purpose at this time or not. You may be a long way from realization of your definite chief aim, but if you will kindle the fire of enthusiasm in your heart, and keep it burning, before very long the obstacles that now stand in the way of your attainment of that purpose will melt away as if by magic, and you will find yourself in possession of power that you did not know you possessed.

HOW ENTHUSIASM AFFECTS OTHERS

We come now to the discussion of one of the most important subjects of this course—suggestion. Suggestion is the principle through which your words and your acts and even your state of mind influence others.

When your own mind is vibrating at a high rate because it has been stimulated with enthusiasm, that vibration registers in the minds of all within its radius, and especially in the minds of those with whom you come in close contact.

When a public speaker "senses" the audience is "en rapport" (in harmony) with him or her, they are merely recognizing that their own enthusiasm has influenced the minds of the listeners until the listeners' minds are vibrating in harmony with the speaker's own.

When a salesperson senses that the "psychological" moment for closing a sale has arrived, he or she merely feels the effect of their own enthusiasm as it influences the mind of the prospective buyer and places that mind "en rapport" with the salesperson's own.

If you accept the principle of telepathy (the communication of thought from one mind to another without the aid of signs, symbols, or sounds) as a reality, you of course understand why enthusiasm is contagious and why it influences all within its radius.

The preceding sections are adapted from the chapter titled Enthusiasm, in *Law of Success*. The following definition is from the chapter titled Self-Confidence, also in *Law of Success*:

THE LAW OF MENTAL TELEPATHY

Others will believe in you only when you believe in yourself. They will "tune in" on your thoughts and feel toward you just as you feel toward yourself. The law of mental telepathy takes care of this. You are continuously broadcasting what you think of yourself, and if you have no faith in yourself, others will pick up your thoughts and mistake them for their own.

The following resumes the adapted excerpt from the chapter titled Enthusiasm, in *Law of Success*:

MANIFESTING A THOUGHT IN ANOTHERS MIND

Suggestion is one of the most subtle and powerful principles of psychology. You are making use of it in all that you do and say and think. But, unless you understand the difference between negative suggestion and positive suggestion, you may be using it in such a way that it is bringing you defeat instead of success.

The human mind is a marvelous piece of machinery! One of its outstanding characteristics is that all impressions which reach it, either through outside suggestion or autosuggestion, are recorded together in groups which harmonize in nature. The negative impressions are stored away, all in one portion of the brain, while the positive impressions are stored in another portion. When one of these impressions (or past experiences) is called into the conscious mind through the principle of memory, there is a tendency to recall with it all others of a similar nature, just as raising one link of a chain brings up other links with it.

For example, anything that causes a feeling of doubt to arise in a person's mind is sufficient to call forth all of their experiences that caused them to become doubtful. If a person is asked by a stranger to cash a check, he or she may immediately remember having cashed checks that were not good, or of having heard of others who did so. Through the law of association, all similar emotions, experiences, and sense impressions that reach the mind are filed away together, so that the recalling of one tends to bring back to memory all the others.

This principle applies to and controls every sense impression that is lodged in the human mind. Take the feeling of fear, for example. The moment we permit a single emotion that is related to fear to reach the conscious mind, it calls with it all of its unsavory relations. A feeling of courage cannot claim the attention of the conscious mind while a feeling of fear is there. One or the other must dominate. They make poor roommates because they do not harmonize in nature. Like attracts like. Every thought held in the conscious mind has a tendency to draw to it other thoughts of a similar nature.

Deliberately place in your own mind, through the principle of autosuggestion, the ambition to succeed through the aid of a definite chief aim, and notice how quickly all of your past experiences will become stimulated and aroused to action on your behalf.

If you wish to plant a suggestion "deeply," mix it generously with enthusiasm, for enthusiasm is the fertilizer that will ensure its rapid growth as well as its permanency.

The following is excerpted and adapted from the chapter titled Self-Control, in *Law of Success*:

SELF-CONTROL

No other animal has ever been endowed with such self-control as you possess. You have been endowed with the power to use the most highly organized form of energy known—that of *thought*. It is not improbable that thought is the closest connecting link there is between the material, physical things of this world and the world of Divinity.

You have not only the power to think, but what is a thousand times more important still, you have the power to control your thoughts and direct them to do your bidding!

We are coming now to the really important part of this lesson. Read slowly and meditatively.

I approach this part of the lesson almost with fear and trembling, for it brings us face to face with a subject that but few are qualified to discuss with reasonable intelligence.

I repeat, you have the power to control your thoughts and direct them to do your bidding!

Your brain may be likened to a dynamo, in that it generates or sets into motion the mysterious energy called thought. The stimuli that set your brain into action are of two sorts; one is autosuggestion and the other is suggestion.

You can select the material out of which your thinking is produced, and that is autosuggestion (or self-suggestion). You can permit others to select the material out of which your thinking is produced, and that is suggestion.

It is a humiliating fact that most thought is produced by the outside suggestions of others, and it is more humiliating still to have to admit that the majority of us accept this suggestion without examining it or questioning its soundness. We read the daily papers as though every word were based on fact. We are swayed by the gossip and idle chatter of others as though every word were true.

Thought is the only thing over which you have absolute control. Yet you permit other people to enter the sacred mansion of your mind and there deposit, through suggestion, their troubles and woes, adversities and falsehoods, just as though you did not have the power to close the door and keep them out.

You have within your control the power to select the material that constitutes the dominating thoughts of your mind, and just as surely as you are reading these lines, those thoughts which dominate your mind will bring you success or failure, according to their nature.

The fact that thought is the only thing over which you have absolute control is of most profound significance. It strongly suggests that thought is your nearest approach to Divinity, on this earthly plane. Thought is your most important tool; the one with which you may shape your worldly destiny according to your own liking.

Self-control is solely a matter of *thought control!*

Please read the foregoing sentence aloud. Read it thoughtfully and meditate over it before reading further, because it is, without doubt, the most important single sentence of this entire course.

You are studying this course, presumably, because you are earnestly seeking truth and understanding sufficient to enable you to attain some high station in life.

You are searching for the magic key that will unlock the door to the source of power. And yet you have the key in your own hands, and you may make use of it the moment you learn to *control your thoughts.*

Place in your own mind, through the principle of autosuggestion, the positive, constructive thoughts that harmonize with your definite chief aim in life, and your mind will transform those thoughts into physical reality and hand them back to you, as a finished product.

This is thought control. When you deliberately choose the thoughts that dominate your mind, and firmly refuse admittance to outside suggestion, you are exercising self-control in its highest and most efficient form. Human beings are the only animals that can do this.

The point I wish to clearly establish in this lesson is that thought, whether accurate or inaccurate, is the most highly organized functioning power of your mind, and that you are but the sum total of your dominating or most prominent thoughts.

HOW DO YOU CONTROL YOUR THOUGHTS?

A student in one of my classes once asked how to control your thoughts when in a state of intense anger. I replied: "In exactly the same way you would change your manner and the tone of your voice if you were in a heated argument with a member of your family and heard the doorbell ring, warning that company had arrived. You would control yourself because you would desire to do so."

If you have ever been in a similar predicament, where you found it necessary to cover up your real feelings and change the expression on your face quickly, you know how easily it can be done. You also know that it can be done because you *want* to do it!

Behind all achievement, behind all self-control, behind all thought control, is that magic something called desire.

Don't say it can't be done, or that you are different from these and thousands of others who have achieved noteworthy success in every worthy calling. If you are "different" it is only in this respect: *they desired the object of their achievement with more depth and intensity than you desire yours.*

The following is excerpted and adapted from the chapter titled A Definite Chief Aim, in *Law of Success*:

Whatever you want you may get—if you want it with sufficient intensity, and keep on wanting it, providing the object wanted is one within reason, and you *actually believe you will get it!* There is a difference, however, between merely wishing for something and *actually believing* you will get it.

Those who believe that they can achieve the object of their definite chief aim do not recognize the word *impossible.* Neither do they acknowledge a temporary defeat. They know they are going to succeed, and if one plan fails they quickly replace it with another plan.

Every noteworthy achievement met with some sort of temporary setback before success came. Edison conducted more than ten thousand experiments before he succeeded in making the first talking machine record the words "Mary had a little lamb."

If there is one word that should stand out in your mind in connection with this lesson, it is the word *persistence.*

You now have within your possession the key to achievement. You have but to unlock the door to the Temple of Knowledge and walk in. But you must go to the temple; it will not come to you.

Everything has a price. There is no such possibility as "something for nothing." You are jockeying with nature in her highest and noblest form. Nature cannot be tricked or cheated. She will give up to you the object of your struggles only after you have paid her price—which is continuous, unyielding, persistent effort!

The remainder of this section is adapted from the chapter in *Think and Grow Rich* titled Persistence: The Sustained Effort Necessary to Induce Faith.

Lack of persistence is one of the major causes of failure. Moreover, my experience with thousands of people has proved that lack of persistence is a weakness common to the majority of people. However, it is a weakness that may be overcome by effort. The ease with which lack of persistence may be conquered will depend entirely upon the intensity of your desire—the starting point of all achievement. Keep this constantly in mind.

Weak desires bring weak results, just as a small amount of fire makes a small amount of heat. If you are lacking in persistence, this weakness may be remedied by building a stronger fire under your desires.

The eagerness with which you follow these instructions will indicate clearly how much or how little you really desire to accumulate money. If you find that you are indifferent, you may be sure that you have not yet acquired the "money consciousness" that you must possess before you can be sure of accumulating a fortune.

Fortunes gravitate to those whose minds have been prepared to attract them, just as surely as water gravitates to the ocean.

Occasional effort to apply the rules will be of no value to you. To get results, you must apply all of the rules until they become a fixed habit with you. In no other way can you develop the necessary "money consciousness."

Just as money is attracted to those who have deliberately set their mind on it, poverty is attracted to those whose mind is open to it. And although money consciousness must be developed intentionally, poverty consciousness develops without conscious application of the habits favorable to it. Poverty consciousness will seize the mind that is not occupied with money consciousness.

FEAR OF CRITICISM KILLS IDEAS

Too many people refuse to set high goals for themselves, because they fear the criticism of relatives and friends who may say, "Don't aim so high, people will think you are crazy."

When Andrew Carnegie suggested that I devote twenty years to the organization of a philosophy of individual achievement, my first impulse was fear of what people might say. My next instinct was to create excuses, all of them traceable to the fear of criticism. Something inside of me said, "You can't do it—the job is too big and requires too much time—what will your relatives think of you?—how will you earn a living?—no one has ever organized a philosophy of success, what right have you to believe you can do it?—who are you, anyway, to aim so high?—remember your humble birth—what do you know about philosophy?—people will think you are crazy (and they did)—why hasn't some other person done this before now?"

These and many other questions flashed into my mind. It seemed as if the whole world had suddenly turned its attention to me with the purpose of ridiculing me into giving up all desire to carry out Mr. Carnegie's suggestion.

Later in life, after having analyzed thousands of people, I discovered that most ideas are stillborn. To grow, ideas need the breath of life injected into them through definite plans of immediate action. The time to nurse an idea is at the time of its birth. Every minute it lives gives it a better chance of surviving. The fear of criticism is what kills most ideas that never reach the planning and action stage.

HOW TO DEVELOP PERSISTENCE

There are four simple steps that lead to the habit of persistence. They call for no great amount of intelligence, no particular amount of education, and little time or effort:

1. A definite purpose backed by a burning desire for its fulfillment.

2. A definite plan, expressed in continuous action.

3. A mind closed tightly against all negative and discouraging influences, including negative suggestions of relatives, friends, and acquaintances.

4. A friendly alliance with one or more persons who will encourage you to follow through with your plan. This is dealt with further in the chapter on Master Mind alliances.

HOW TO MASTER DIFFICULTIES

What mystical power gives people of persistence the capacity to master difficulties? Does the quality of persistence set up in your mind some form of spiritual, mental, or chemical activity that gives you access to supernatural forces?

These questions were in my mind as I watched Henry Ford start from scratch and build an industrial empire, with little more than persistence. Or Thomas A. Edison who, with less than three months of schooling, became the world's leading inventor.

I had the opportunity to analyze both Mr. Edison and Mr. Ford, up close, year by year, over a long period of time. So I speak from actual knowledge when I say that I found no quality except persistence, in either of them, that even remotely suggested the major source of their stupendous achievements.

If you make an impartial study of the prophets, philosophers, and religious leaders of the past, you will come to the inevitable conclusion that persistence, concentration of effort, and definiteness of purpose were the major sources of their achievements.

Chapter 6

Autosuggestion

& the Subconscious Mind

The subconscious mind consists of a field of consciousness in which every thought that reaches the mind, through any of the five senses, is classified and recorded. The subconscious mind receives and files sense impressions or thoughts regardless of their nature.

You may plant in your subconscious mind any plan, thought, or purpose that you desire to translate into its physical or monetary equivalent. Those desires that have been mixed with emotional feeling, and faith, are the ones that are strongest. Therefore they are the first to which the subconscious responds.

The subconscious mind works day and night, and in some way which is not fully understood, the subconscious seems able to draw upon the forces of Infinite Intelligence for the power to transmute your desires into their physical equivalent. And it does it in the most straightforward and practical way.

You cannot entirely control your subconscious mind, but you can hand over to it any plan, desire, or purpose that you wish transformed into concrete form.

From my research, I have concluded that the subconscious mind is the connecting link between the finite mind of man and Infinite Intelligence. It is the intermediary through which you may draw upon the forces of Infinite Intelligence. Only the subconscious mind contains the secret process by which mental impulses (thoughts) are modified and changed into their spiritual (energy) equivalent. It alone is the medium through which prayer (desire) may be transmitted to the source capable of answering prayer (Infinite Intelligence).

The preceding is from *Think and Grow Rich,* and is excerpted and adapted from the opening to the chapter titled The Subconscious Mind: The Connecting Link.

The following, also from *Think and Grow Rich,* is excerpted and adapted from the chapter titled Autosuggestion: The Medium for Influencing the Subconscious Mind.

Autosuggestion is a term that applies to all suggestions and all self-administered stimuli that reach your mind through the five senses. Stated in another way, autosuggestion is self-suggestion. It is the way of communicating between that part of the mind where conscious thought takes place, and that which serves as the seat of action for the subconscious mind.

Through the dominating thoughts that you permit to remain in your conscious mind (it doesn't matter whether these thoughts are negative or positive), the principle of autosuggestion reaches the subconscious mind and influences it with these thoughts.

Nature has built human beings so that, through our five senses, we can have control over the material that reaches our subconscious mind. However, this does not mean that we always exercise this control. In the great majority of instances we do not exercise it, which explains why so many people go through life in poverty.

Recall what I said about the subconscious mind resembling a fertile garden, in which weeds will grow if the seeds of more desirable crops are not sown. Autosuggestion is the way you may feed your subconscious on creative thoughts, or you can, by neglecting it, permit thoughts of a destructive nature to find their way into this rich garden of the mind.

You were instructed, in the last of the six steps described in the chapter on Desire, to read aloud twice daily the written statement of your desire for money. You were also directed to see and feel yourself already in possession of the money. By following these instructions, you communicate the object of your desire directly to your subconscious mind in a spirit of absolute faith. Through repetition of this procedure, you will create thought habits that reinforce your efforts to transmute desire into its monetary equivalent.

Remember, when reading aloud the statement of your desire (through which you will develop a "money consciousness"), that the mere reading of the words is of no consequence— unless you mix emotion, or feeling, with your words. If you repeat a million times the famous Emile Coué formula, "Day by day in every way I am getting better and better," without mixing emotion and faith with your words, you will experience no desirable results.

Your subconscious mind recognizes and acts only upon thoughts that have been well mixed with emotion or feeling.

The following is excerpted and adapted from the chapter titled The Subconscious Mind, from *Think and Grow Rich*.

MAKE YOUR POSITIVE EMOTIONS WORK FOR YOU

The subconscious mind is more susceptible to influence by thoughts mixed with feeling or emotion than it is by thoughts originating solely in the reasoning portion of the mind. In fact, there is much evidence to support the theory that only emotionalized thoughts have any real influence on the subconscious. It is a fact that emotions or feelings rule the majority of people. If it is true that the subconscious responds better and faster to thoughts well mixed with emotion, it is essential to become familiar with the more important of the emotions.

There are seven major positive emotions and seven major negative emotions. The negatives get into your thoughts naturally and go directly to your subconscious without any help from you. The positive emotions must be injected by you, through the principle of autosuggestion, into the thought impulses that you wish to pass on to your subconscious mind.

These emotions, or feeling impulses, may be likened to yeast in a loaf of bread. They are the action element which transforms thought impulses from the passive to the active state. That is why thought impulses that have been well mixed with emotion are acted upon more readily than thought impulses originating in "cold reason."

You are preparing yourself to influence and control the "inner audience" of your subconscious mind in order to hand over to it the desire for money, which you wish transmuted into its physical, monetary equivalent. It is essential, therefore, that you understand the method of approach to this "inner audience." You must speak its language. It understands best the language of emotion or feeling.

Following are the seven major positive emotions and the seven major negative emotions. I am listing them here so that you may draw upon the positives, and avoid the negatives, when giving instructions to your subconscious mind.

The Seven Major Positive Emotions

- The emotion of desire
- The emotion of faith
- The emotion of love
- The emotion of sex
- The emotion of enthusiasm
- The emotion of romance
- The emotion of hope

There are other positive emotions, but these are the seven most powerful and the ones most commonly used in creative effort. Master these seven emotions (they can be mastered only by use) and the other positive emotions will be at your command when you need them. Remember that you are studying a book that is intended to help you develop a "money consciousness" by filling your mind with positive emotions.

The Seven Major Negative Emotions to be Avoided

- The emotion of fear
- The emotion of jealousy
- The emotion of hatred
- The emotion of revenge
- The emotion of greed
- The emotion of superstition
- The emotion of anger

Positive and negative emotions cannot occupy the mind at the same time. One or the other must dominate. It is your responsibility to make sure that positive emotions constitute the dominating influence of your mind. That is where the law of habit will help you. Form the habit of applying and using the positive emotions. Eventually they will dominate your mind so completely that the negatives cannot enter it.

Only by following these instructions literally, and continuously, can you gain control over your subconscious mind. The presence of a single negative in your conscious mind is sufficient to destroy all chances of constructive aid from your subconscious mind.

The following is excerpted from the chapter The Subconscious Mind: The Connecting Link, in *Think and Grow Rich*:

HOW TO ENERGIZE YOUR SUBCONSCIOUS MIND FOR CREATIVE EFFORT

The possibilities of what you can do when you connect creative effort with the subconscious mind are stupendous. They inspire me with awe.

I never approach the discussion of the subconscious mind without a feeling of littleness and inferiority due to the fact that man's entire stock of knowledge on this subject is so pitifully limited.

First, you must accept as a reality the existence of the subconscious mind and what it can do for you. This will enable you to understand its possibilities as a medium for transmuting your desires into their physical or monetary equivalent, and then you will comprehend the full significance of the instructions given in the chapter on Desire. You will also understand the importance of making your desires clear and putting them in writing. You will understand, as well, the necessity of persistence in carrying out instructions.

The principles that are the basis of this book are the stimuli with which you acquire the ability to reach and to influence your subconscious mind. Do not become discouraged if you cannot do this on your first attempt. Remember that the subconscious mind can be directed only through habit. You have not yet had time to master faith. Be patient. Be persistent.

Many statements in the chapters on faith are repeated here for the benefit of your subconscious mind. Remember that your subconscious mind functions whether you make any effort to influence it or not. This means that thoughts of fear, poverty, and all negative ideas will affect your subconscious mind unless you master these impulses and give it more desirable food on which it may feed.

The subconscious mind will not remain idle. If you don't plant desires in your subconscious mind, it will feed on the thoughts that reach it as the result of your neglect.

Both negative and positive thoughts are reaching your subconscious mind continuously. These thoughts come from four sources: (1) consciously from other people, (2) your subconscious, (3) subconsciously from other people, and (4) Infinite Intelligence.

Every day all kinds of thought impulses are reaching your subconscious mind without your knowledge. Some of these impulses are negative, some are positive. Right now you should be specifically trying to shut off the flow of negative impulses, and actively working to influence your subconscious through positive impulses of desire.

When you achieve this, you will possess the key that unlocks the door to your subconscious mind. Moreover, you will control that door so completely that no undesirable thought may influence your subconscious mind.

Everything that you create begins in the form of a thought impulse. You can create nothing that you do not first conceive as a thought. Through the aid of the imagination, thoughts may be assembled into plans. The imagination, when under your control, may be used to create plans or purposes that lead to success in your chosen occupation.

All thoughts that you want to turn into success, and have planted in the subconscious mind, must pass through the imagination and be mixed with faith (your complete belief that you are capable of accomplishing the task). The "mixing" of faith with a plan, or purpose, intended for submission to the subconscious mind can only be done through the imagination.

Chapter 7

Imagination & Infinite Intelligence

Imagination is the workshop of the human mind, wherein old ideas and established facts may be reassembled into new combinations and put to new uses.

If you have mastered the preceding lessons, you know that the materials out of which you built your definite chief aim were assembled and combined in your imagination. You also know that self-confidence, initiative, and leadership must be created in your imagination before they can become a reality, for it is in the workshop of your imagination that you will put the principle of autosuggestion into operation in creating these necessary qualities.

This lesson on imagination might be called the "hub" of this course, because every other lesson of the course leads to this lesson and makes use of the principle upon which it is based, just as all the telephone wires lead to the exchange office for their source of power. You will never have a definite purpose in life, you will never have self-confidence, you will never have initiative and leadership unless you first create these qualities in your imagination and see yourself in possession of them.

Just as the oak tree develops from the germ that lies in the acorn, and the bird develops from the germ that lies asleep in the egg, so will your material achievements grow out of the organized plans that you create in your imagination. First comes the thought; then organization of that thought into ideas and plans; then transformation of those plans into reality. The beginning, as you will observe, is in your imagination.

The preceding is how Napoleon Hill opened the chapter titled Imagination, in *Law of Success*. The following is adapted from the opening of the corresponding chapter in *Think and Grow Rich*.

The imagination is literally the workshop where all plans are created. It is where the impulse, the desire, is given shape, form, and action through the aid of the imaginative faculty of the mind. It has been said that we can create anything that we can imagine.

The imaginative faculty functions in two forms. One form is known as "synthetic imagination" and the other as "creative imagination."

Synthetic Imagination: Through this faculty you arrange old concepts, ideas, or plans into new combinations. Synthesized imagination does not create anything new. It works with the material of experience, education, and observation.

Creative Imagination: It is through creative imagination that the finite human mind has direct communication with Infinite Intelligence, the faculty through which "hunches" and "inspirations" are received.

The two names that Napoleon Hill has chosen to identify the forms of imagination have proven to be somewhat misleading. Generally speaking, today the word *creative* implies something better than the word *synthesized,* and most people would assume from the names that using your creative imagination is better than your synthesized imagination. That is not what Hill meant.

SYNTHETIC IMAGINATION

To clarify, the most creative people in the world utilize synthetic imagination most of the time to come up with their best ideas. Your synthetic imagination is what you are using when you rack your brain and call upon everything you know to come up with an idea or a solution to a problem. Synthesizing, or putting the right things together in the right way, is the height of creativity. That's what scientists, cooks, inventors, mechanics, songwriters, salespeople, students, business managers, and just about everyone else does when they are using their head and working to the best of their ability.

Although using synthesized imagination is indeed a creative process, and part of the process is bringing to your mind other "like ideas," this is not quite the way that the Law of Attraction means "like attracts like."

CREATIVE IMAGINATION

On the other hand, what Hill calls "creative imagination" involves tapping into something beyond the information and ideas you have in your mind. You are using creative imagination when you get a flash of insight or inspiration that comes to you completely out of the blue. At the most rarified level, it is what scientists and inventors tap into when they discover or create something that was previously unknown. More commonly, it is when you get a hunch, a gut feeling, or a premonition about something that turns out to be right, but you had no way of knowing in advance that it would happen.

It is because of the relationship between "creative" imagination and Infinite Intelligence that the subject of imagination is included in this exploration of the Carnegie secret and the Law of Attraction.

USING YOUR CREATIVE IMAGINATION

The great leaders of business, industry, and finance, and the great artists, musicians, poets, and writers became great because they developed the faculty of creative imagination.

You are engaged in trying to turn your desire into its physical or monetary counterpart, and there are laws of nature that can help you. By describing these principles from every conceivable angle, I hope to reveal to you the secret through which every great fortune has been accumulated. Strange and paradoxical as it may seem, the "secret" is not a secret. It is made obvious in the earth, the stars, the planets, in the elements above and around us, in every blade of grass, and every form of life within our vision.

As far as science has been able to determine, the entire universe consists of but four things: time, space, matter and energy. Moreover—and this statement is of stupendous importance—this earth, every one of the billions of individual cells of your body, and every subatomic particle of matter, began as an intangible form of energy. Through the combination of energy and matter has been created everything perceptible, from the largest star in the heavens down to and including man himself.

Desire is a thought impulse. Thought impulses are forms of energy. When you begin the process of acquiring money by using the thought impulse of desire, you are drafting into your service the same "stuff" that nature used in creating this earth, as well as every material form in the universe including your body and your brain in which the thought impulses function.

It is by this faculty of creative imagination that truly new ideas are handed over to mankind. It is through this faculty that we get hunches, and that we pick up "vibrations" from other people, and in that way tune in the subconscious minds of others.

Much of what is explained in the preceding section is often referred to as the "sixth sense." More often than not, these references are made in a negative fashion, the implication being that such things are on a par with magic acts and carnival mind readers. Napoleon Hill acknowledges the criticism and deals with the issue head-on in the following collection of short excerpts taken from various chapters in *Think and Grow Rich*:

I am not a believer in, nor an advocate of, "miracles," for the simple reason that I have enough knowledge of nature to understand that nature never deviates from her established laws. However, I believe that some of nature's laws are so incomprehensible that they produce what *appear* to be miracles. The sixth sense comes as near to being a miracle as anything I have ever experienced.

This much I do know—that there is a power, or a First Cause, or an Intelligence, which permeates every atom of matter and embraces every unit of energy perceptible to man. I know that this Infinite Intelligence is the thing that converts acorns into oak trees, causes water to flow downhill in response to the law of gravity, follows night with day and winter with summer, each maintaining its proper place and relationship to the other. Through the philosophy explained in this book, this Intelligence can help turn your desires into material form. I know this because I have experimented with it—and I have experienced it.

Somewhere in the cell-structure of the brain is something that receives the vibrations of thought ordinarily called hunches. So far, science has not discovered where this sixth sense is located, but this is not important. The fact remains that human beings do receive accurate knowledge through sources other than the physical senses.

This sixth sense is creative imagination. Creative imagination is the direct link between your finite mind and what I have termed Infinite Intelligence. All revelations, and all discoveries of basic or new principles in the field of invention, take place through the faculty of creative imagination.

When ideas, concepts, or hunches flash into your mind, they can only have come from one or more of the following sources:

1. From the mind of some other person who has just released the thought, idea, or concept, through conscious thought

2. Your subconscious mind, which stores every thought and impression that ever reached your brain through any of the five senses

3. From another person's subconscious storehouse

4. Infinite Intelligence

There are no other possible sources from which "inspired" ideas or "hunches" may be received.

In the following section, adapted from the chapter titled Imagination, in *Law of Success,* Napoleon Hill provides more detail about his theory of the way in which your creative imagination acts as a "receiver." In doing so, Hill uses the term *telepathy,* but by the way he uses it, he is not referring to some mystical psychic phenomenon.

Hill's approach to telepathy is purely practical. The fact is that in real life we all get hunches and we all pick up "vibes" from some people. If we all have these experiences, and neither science nor psychology has yet to come up with an explanation of how these ideas get into our minds, Hill's theory of Infinite Intelligence provides a reasonable common-sense answer.

Through its interpretative capacity, the imagination has one power not generally attributed to it: the power to register vibrations and thought waves that are put into motion from outside sources, just as the radio receiver picks up the vibrations of sound. The principle through which this interpretative capacity of the imagination functions is called telepathy—the communication of thought from one mind to another, at long or short distances, without the aid of physical or mechanical appliances.

I will devote no time to proving that telepathy is a reality. To make this description understandable we must simply accept the principle of telepathy, in the sense that every thought we release is registering itself in the minds of other people.

Telepathy can be an important factor to a student who is preparing to make effective use of imagination, because this telepathic capacity of the imagination is constantly picking up thought waves and vibrations of every description. So-called "snap judgments" and "hunches," which prompt you to form an opinion or decide upon a course of action that is not in harmony with logic and reason, are usually the result of stray thought waves that have registered in the imagination.

Consider, for example, what happens when a salesperson who lacks confidence in himself, and in his goods, walks in to see a prospective buyer. Whether or not the prospective buyer is conscious of it, his or her imagination immediately "senses" that lack of confidence in the salesperson's mind. The salesperson's own thoughts are actually undermining his own efforts.

The principle of telepathy and the law of attraction, through which like attracts like, explain many a failure. If the mind has a tendency to attract those thought vibrations which harmonize with the dominating thoughts of a given mind, you can easily understand why a negative mind that dwells on failure and lacks self-confidence would not attract a positive mind that is dominated by thoughts of success.

The following section, excerpted from the chapter Accurate Thinking, in *Law of Success*, offers a comprehensive recap of the interconnection between creative imagination, the subconscious mind, and Infinite Intelligence:

The average person is totally lost the moment they get beyond what they can comprehend with the aid of their five physical senses of seeing, hearing, feeling, smelling, and tasting. Infinite Intelligence works through none of these agencies and we cannot invoke its aid through any of them.

The only way to use the power of Infinite Intelligence is through creative thought.

The subconscious mind is the intermediary between the conscious thinking mind and Infinite Intelligence, and you can invoke the aid of Infinite Intelligence only through the medium of the subconscious mind, by giving it clear instructions as to what you want. Autosuggestion is the way in which you may register in your subconscious mind a description or plan of what you wish to create or acquire in physical form.

Here you become familiar with the psychological reason for a definite chief aim. If you have not already seen the importance of creating a definite chief aim as the object of your life's work, you will undoubtedly do so before this lesson has been mastered.

Knowing from my own experience how little I understood about such terms as *subconscious mind, autosuggestion,* and *creative thought,* throughout this course I have described these terms through every conceivable simile and illustration, with the object of making their meaning and the method of their application so clear that no student of this course can possibly fail to understand.

An outstanding characteristic of the subconscious mind is that it records the suggestions that you send it through autosuggestion, and it invokes the aid of Infinite Intelligence in translating these suggestions into their natural physical form. It is important that you understand this last sentence, for if you fail to understand it, you are likely to also fail to understand the importance of the very foundation upon which this entire course is built—the principle of Infinite Intelligence.

Study carefully, thoughtfully, and with meditation, the entire preceding paragraph.

An outstanding characteristic of the subconscious mind is that it accepts and acts upon all suggestions that reach it, whether they are constructive or destructive, and whether they come from the outside or from your own conscious mind.

You can see, therefore, how essential it is to carefully select what you will pass on to your subconscious mind through autosuggestion. You can see why you must search diligently for facts, and why you cannot afford to listen to the slanderer or the scandalmonger, for to do so would be poisonous to the subconscious mind and ruinous to creative thought.

The subconscious mind may be likened to the sensitive plate of a camera on which the picture of any object placed before the camera will be recorded. The plate does not choose the sort of picture to be recorded on it; it records anything that reaches it through the lens.

The conscious mind may be likened to the shutter, which shuts off the light from the sensitized plate, permitting nothing to reach it except for what the operator wishes to reach it.

The part that you must play is clear. You select the picture to be recorded (your definite chief aim), then you fix your conscious mind on this purpose with such intensity that it communicates with the subconscious mind, through autosuggestion, and registers that picture. You then begin to watch for and to expect manifestations of physical realization of the subject of that picture.

Bear in mind that you do not sit down and wait, nor do you go to bed and sleep, with the expectation of awaking to find that Infinite Intelligence has showered you with the object of your definite chief aim. You must work to make it happen, with full faith and confidence that natural ways and means for the attainment of the object of your definite purpose will open to you at the proper time and in a suitable manner.

Infinite Intelligence will not build you a home and deliver that home to you, ready to enter, but Infinite Intelligence will open the way and provide the necessary means with which *you* may build your own house.

Infinite Intelligence will not command your bank to place a definite sum of money in your account, just because you suggested this to your subconscious mind, but Infinite Intelligence will open to you the way in which you may earn or borrow that money and place it in your account yourself.

Infinite Intelligence will not throw out the present incumbent of the White House and make you president instead. But Infinite Intelligence would most likely, under the proper circumstances, influence you to prepare yourself to fill that position and then help you to attain it through regular methods of procedure.

Do not rely on miracles for the attainment of the object of your definite chief aim; rely on the power of Infinite Intelligence to guide you, through natural channels and with the aid of natural laws, toward its attainment. Do not expect Infinite Intelligence to bring to you the object of your definite chief aim. Instead, expect it to direct you toward that object.

As a beginner, do not expect Infinite Intelligence to move quickly on your behalf. But as you become more adept in the use of the principle of autosuggestion, and as your faith and understanding grow, you will see the realization of your definite chief aim and its translation into physical reality.

You did not walk the first time you tried, but as you matured you walked without effort. Keep this in mind and you will understand why you cannot reasonably expect Infinite Intelligence to circumvent natural laws and provide you with its full knowledge and power until you have prepared yourself to use this knowledge and power.

I am fully aware that much of what I am proposing will not be understood or believed by the beginner. I remember my own experiences at the start. However, as the evolutionary process carries on its work—and it will do so; make no mistake about this—all the principles described in this and all other lessons of this course will become as familiar to you as did the multiplication table after you had mastered it. And what is of greater importance still, these principles will work with the same unvarying certainty as does the principle of multiplication.

I remind you to familiarize yourself with the four major factors in this lesson: (1) autosuggestion, (2) the subconscious mind, (3) creative thought, and (4) Infinite Intelligence. They are the four roadways over which you must travel in your upward climb in quest of knowledge.

You understand what is meant by the terms *autosuggestion* and *subconscious mind.* Let us again make sure that you also understand what is meant by the term *creative thought.* It means thought of a positive, nondestructive, creative nature.

Remember, it is in your subconscious mind that the seed of your definite chief aim is planted, and it is with creative thought that you awaken that seed into growth and maturity. Your subconscious mind will not germinate the seed of your definite chief aim, nor will Infinite Intelligence translate that purpose into physical reality, if you fill your mind with hatred, envy, jealousy, selfishness, and greed. These negative thoughts will choke out the seed of your definite purpose.

Creative thought presupposes that you will keep your mind in a state of expectancy of attainment of the object of your definite chief aim; that you will have full faith and confidence in its attainment in due course and in due order.

As a final word, the following is excerpted from the chapter The Mystery of Sex Transmutation, in *Think and Grow Rich*:

The more you use your creative faculty, the more alert and receptive it becomes to factors originating outside your conscious mind. And the more this creative faculty is used, the more you will rely upon it for your thoughts and ideas. This faculty can be cultivated and developed only through use.

What we generally refer to as our "conscience" operates entirely through the faculty of the sixth sense.

The great artists, writers, musicians, and poets become great because they acquire the habit of relying upon the "still small voice" that speaks from within, through their creative imagination. Anyone with a keen imagination knows that some of their best ideas come through so-called "hunches."

Chapter 8

Concentration
&
Creative Visualization

The following is excerpted and adapted from the chapter titled Concentration, in *Law of Success*:

This lesson holds a keystone position in this course, because the psychological law upon which it is based is of vital importance to every other lesson of the course.

Let me first define the word *concentration* as it is used in this lesson: "Concentration is the act of focusing the mind on a given desire until ways and means for its realization have been worked out and successfully put into operation."

Two important laws enter into the act of concentrating the mind on a given desire. One is the law of autosuggestion and the other is the law of habit.

Habit grows out of environment—the sum total of all sources by which you are influenced through the five senses of seeing, hearing, smelling, tasting, and feeling—and out of doing the same thing in the same way over and over again, out of repetition, out of thinking the same thoughts over and over.

The human mind draws from its surroundings the material out of which thought is created. Habit crystallizes this thought into a permanent fixture, storing it away in the subconscious mind where it becomes a vital part of your personality and silently influences your actions, forms your prejudices and biases, and controls your opinions.

We begin to see, therefore, the importance of selecting our environment with the greatest of care, because environment is the mental feeding ground out of which the food that goes into our minds is extracted.

CONCENTRATION IS CREATIVE VISUALIZATION

This brings us to an appropriate place at which to describe the method through which you may apply the principles directly and indirectly related to the subject of concentration. I call this method the Magic Key to Success, and this magic key *is* concentration.

Through the aid of this magic key, we have unlocked the secret doors to all of the world's great inventions. Through its magic powers, all of our great geniuses of the past have been developed.

Concentration means the ability, through fixed habit and practice, to keep your mind on one subject until you have thoroughly familiarized yourself with that subject and mastered it. It means the ability to control your attention and focus it on a given problem until you have solved that problem. It means the ability to throw off the effects of the habits you wish to discard, and the power to build new habits. It means complete self-mastery.

Concentration is the ability to think as you wish to think, the ability to control your thoughts and direct them to a definite end, and the ability to organize your knowledge into a plan of action that is sound and workable.

You can readily see that in concentrating your mind on your definite chief aim in life, you must cover many closely related subjects that blend into each other and complete the main subject on which you are concentrating. Ambition and desire are the major factors that enter into the act of successful concentration. Without these factors the magic key is useless, and the main reason why so few people make use of this key is that most people lack ambition, and desire nothing in particular.

Desire whatever you may, and if your desire is within reason and if it is strong enough, the magic key of concentration will help you to attain it. There are many scientists and research psychologists who believe that the power of prayer operates through the principle of concentration on the attainment of a deeply seated desire.

Nothing was ever created by a human being that was not first created in the imagination, through desire, and then transformed into reality through concentration.

Let us put the magic key to a test through the aid of a definite formula.

First you must get rid of skepticism and doubt. There was never an unbeliever who enjoyed the benefits of this magic key. You must *believe* in the test that you are about to make.

Perhaps you have thought about becoming a successful writer, or perhaps a powerful public speaker, or a successful business executive, or an able financier. We will take public speaking as the subject of this test, but you can change that to your own objective. Just remember that you must follow instructions to the letter. On a plain sheet of letter-size paper, write the following:

I am going to become a powerful public speaker because this will enable me to render the world a useful service that is needed—and because it will yield me a financial return that will provide me with the necessary material things of life.

I will concentrate my mind on this desire for ten minutes daily, just before retiring at night and just after arising in the morning, for the purpose of determining just how I shall proceed to transform it into reality.

I know that I can become a powerful and magnetic speaker, therefore I will permit nothing to interfere with my doing so.

Signed . . . .

After signing this pledge, proceed to do as you have given your word you would do. Keep it up until the desired results have been realized.

When you practice the method of concentration, look ahead one, three, five, or even ten years, and see yourself as the most powerful speaker of your time. See, in your imagination, an appropriate income. See yourself in your own home that you have purchased with the proceeds from your efforts as a speaker or lecturer. See yourself in possession of a nice bank account for your retirement. See yourself as a person of influence, due to your great ability as a public speaker. See yourself engaged in a life-calling in which you will not fear the loss of your position.

Paint this picture clearly, through the powers of your imagination, and it will soon become transformed into a beautiful picture of a deeply seated desire. Use this desire as the chief object of your concentration and observe what happens.

You should now understand how the secret of the magic key is concentration. Do not underestimate its power because it did not come to you clothed in mysticism, or because it is described in language that anyone can understand. All great truths are simple in the final analysis, and easily understood. If they are not, they are not *great* truths.

Use the magic key with intelligence, and only for the attainment of worthy ends, and it will bring you enduring happiness and success.

Forget the mistakes you have made and the failures you have experienced. Quit living in the past, for your yesterdays can never return. If your previous efforts have not turned out well, start all over again and make the future tell a story of success.

Make a name for yourself and render the world a great service—through ambition, desire, and concentrated effort.

You can do it if you believe you can!

When you become familiar with the powers of concentration, it becomes clear why it is so important to choose a definite chief aim as the first step in the attainment of enduring success.

The presence of any idea or thought in your consciousness tends to produce an "associated" feeling and urge you to an appropriate or corresponding action. Hold a deeply seated desire in your consciousness, through the principle of concentration, and if you do this with full faith in its realization, that act will attract powers which the entire scientific world has failed to understand or explain.

Concentrate your mind on the attainment of the object of a deeply seated desire, and soon you will attract, through those forces that no one can explain, the material counterparts of that desire.

The following is excerpted and adapted from the chapter titled Autosuggestion: The Medium for Influencing the Subconscious Mind, which appears in *Think and Grow Rich*:

SEE AND FEEL MONEY IN YOUR HANDS

You were instructed previously to read aloud twice daily the written statement of your desire for money. You were also directed to see and feel yourself already in possession of that money. By following these instructions, you communicate the object of your desire directly to your subconscious mind in a spirit of absolute faith. Through repetition, you will create thought habits that reinforce your efforts to transmute desire into its monetary equivalent.

Read these steps again, very carefully, before you proceed any further.

1. Fix in your mind the exact amount of money you desire. It is not sufficient merely to say "I want plenty of money." Be definite about the amount.

2. Determine exactly what you intend to give in return for the money you desire. (There is no such reality as "something for nothing.")

3. Establish a definite date by which you intend to possess the money you desire.

4. Create a definite plan for carrying out your desire, and begin at once, whether you are ready or not, to put this plan into action.

5. Now write it out. Write a clear, concise statement of the amount of money you intend to acquire, name the time limit for its acquisition, state what you intend to give in return for the money, and describe clearly the plan through which you intend to accumulate it.

6. Read your written statement aloud, twice daily. Read it once just before retiring at night, and read it once after arising in the morning. As you read, see and feel and believe yourself already in possession of the money.

Remember, when reading aloud the statement of your desire (through which you will develop a "money consciousness"), that the mere reading of the words is of no consequence—unless you mix emotion, or feeling, with your words. Your subconscious mind recognizes and acts only on thoughts that have been well mixed with emotion or feeling.

This is a fact of such importance as to warrant repetition in practically every chapter. The lack of understanding of this is the main reason that the majority of people who try to apply the principle of autosuggestion get no desirable results.

Plain, unemotional words will have no influence on the subconscious mind. You will get no appreciable results until you learn to reach your subconscious mind with thoughts or spoken words that have been well emotionalized with belief.

Do not become discouraged if you cannot control and direct your emotions the first time you try. Remember, there is no such possibility as something for nothing. You cannot cheat, even if you desire to do so. The price of ability to influence your subconscious mind is persistence in applying the principles described here. You cannot develop the desired ability for a lower price. You, and you alone, must decide whether or not the reward (the money consciousness) is worth the price you must pay for it in effort.

Your ability to use the principle of autosuggestion will depend, very largely, upon your capacity to concentrate on a given desire until that desire becomes a burning obsession.

STRENGTHEN YOUR CONCENTRATION

When you begin to carry out the instructions in the six steps, it will be necessary for you to make use of the principle of concentration. Following are some suggestions for the effective use of concentration.

When you begin the first of the six steps, which instructs you to "fix in your own mind the exact amount of money you desire," close your eyes and hold your thoughts on that amount of money until you can actually see the physical appearance of the money. Do this at least once each day. As you go through these exercises, follow the instructions given in chapter 4 on faith, and see yourself actually in possession of the money.

Here is a most significant fact: The subconscious mind takes any orders given to it in a spirit of absolute faith, and acts upon those orders. But the orders often have to be presented over and over again (repeated positive affirmation) before they are interpreted by the subconscious mind. Because of this, you might consider the possibility of playing a perfectly legitimate "trick" on your subconscious mind. Make it believe (because you believe it) that you *must* have the amount of money you are visualizing. Make it believe that this money is already awaiting your claim, so the subconscious mind must hand over to you practical plans for acquiring the money that is yours.

Give this thought to your imagination and see what your imagination can, or will, do to create practical plans for the accumulation of money through transmutation of your desire.

Do not wait for a definite plan through which you will exchange services or merchandise in return for the money you are visualizing. Just start right now to see yourself in possession of the money, demanding and expecting that your subconscious mind will hand over the plans you need. Be on alert for these plans, and when they appear, put them into action immediately. When the plans do appear, they will probably "flash" into your mind in the form of an inspiration or intuition (from Infinite Intelligence). Treat it with respect, and act upon it as soon as you receive it.

In the fourth of the six steps, you were instructed to "create a definite plan for carrying out your desire, and begin at once to put this plan into action." Do the same thing here. Close your eyes and create in your mind a vivid image of you carrying out the instructions. Do not trust to your "reason" when creating your plan for accumulating money through the transmutation of desire. Your reasoning faculty may be lazy, and if you depend entirely upon it to serve you, it may disappoint you.

When visualizing the money you intend to accumulate, see yourself rendering the service or delivering the merchandise you intend to give in return for this money. This is important!

PUTTING IT TO WORK

The instructions given previously for the steps necessary in your desire for money will now be summarized and blended with the principles covered in this chapter, as follows:

1. Go to some quiet spot where you will not be disturbed or interrupted. Close your eyes and repeat aloud (so that you may hear your own words) the written statement of the amount of money you intend to accumulate. Be specific about the time limit for its accumulation, and a description of the service or merchandise you intend to give in return for the money. As you carry out these instructions, see yourself already in possession of the money.

For example, suppose that you intend to accumulate $50,000 by the first of January, five years from now, and that you intend to give your personal services as a salesperson in return for the money. Your written statement of your purpose should be similar to the following:

By the first day of January, _____, I will have in my possession $50,000, which will come to me in various amounts from time to time in the interim.

In return for this money, I will give the most efficient service of which I am capable. I will give the fullest possible quantity, and the best possible quality, of service as a salesperson of _____ (describe the service or merchandise you intend to sell).

I believe that I will have this money in my possession. My faith is so strong that I can now see this money before my eyes. I can touch it with my hands. It is now awaiting transfer to me at the time and in the proportion that I deliver the service in return for it. I am awaiting a plan for getting this money, and I will follow that plan when it is received.

2. Repeat this night and morning until you can see (in your imagination) the money you intend to accumulate.

3. Place a written copy of your statement where you can see it night and morning, and read it just before retiring and upon arising, until it has been memorized.

Remember, as you carry out these instructions, that you are applying the principle of autosuggestion—for the purpose of giving orders to your subconscious mind. Remember, also, that your subconscious mind will act only upon instructions that are emotionalized and handed over to it with "feeling." Faith is the strongest, and most productive, of the emotions.

These instructions may, at first, seem abstract. Do not let this disturb you. Follow the instructions no matter how abstract or impractical they may appear to be. If you do as you have been instructed, in spirit as well as in act, the time will soon come when a whole new universe of power will unfold to you.

Skepticism, in connection with all new ideas, is characteristic of all human beings. If you follow the instructions, your skepticism will soon be replaced by belief, and belief will become crystallized into absolute faith.

Many philosophers have made the statement that man is the master of his own earthly destiny, but most of them have failed to say why he is the master. The reason man may become the master of himself, and of his environment, is that he has the power to influence his own subconscious mind.

The actual performance of transmuting desire into money is through autosuggestion. That is the principle by which you can reach, and influence, the subconscious mind. The other principles are simply tools with which to apply autosuggestion.

Chapter 9

The Law of
the Master Mind

The following is excerpted and adapted from the chapter A Definite Chief Aim, in *Law of Success*:

Nearly twenty years ago I interviewed Andrew Carnegie for the purpose of writing a story about him. During the interview I asked him to what he attributed his success. With a merry little twinkle in his eyes, he said:

"Young man, before I answer your question, will you please define your term 'success'?"

After waiting until he saw that I was somewhat embarrassed by this request, he continued: "By success you make reference to my money, do you not?"

I assured him that money was the term by which most
people measured success, and he then said: "Oh, well, if you
wish to know how I got my money—*if that is what you call
success*—I will answer your question by saying that we have a
Master Mind here in our business, and that mind is made up
of more than a score of men who constitute my personal staff
of superintendents and managers and accountants and chemists
and other necessary types. No one person in this group is the
Master Mind of which I speak, but the sum total of all the
minds in the group, coordinated, organized, and directed to a
definite end in a spirit of harmonious cooperation, is the power
that got my money for me. No two minds in the group are
exactly alike, but each man in the group does the thing that he
is supposed to do and he does it better than any other person
in the world could do it."

Then and there, the seed out of which this course has since
been developed was sown in my mind. This interview marked
the beginning of years of research which led, finally, to the discovery of the principle of psychology since described as the
Master Mind.

Carnegie's group of men constituted a Master Mind, and
that mind was so well-organized, so well-coordinated, and so
powerful, that it could have accumulated millions of dollars for

Mr. Carnegie in practically any sort of endeavor of a commercial or industrial nature.

The steel business in which that mind was engaged was but an incident in connection with the accumulation of the Carnegie wealth. The same wealth could have been accumulated had the Master Mind been directed in the coal business or the banking business or the grocery business, because behind that mind was power—the sort of power that you may attain when you have organized the faculties of your own mind and allied yourself with other well-organized minds for the attainment of a definite chief aim in life.

A careful checkup with several of Mr. Carnegie's former business associates proves conclusively not only that there *is* such a law as that which has been called the Master Mind, but that this law was the chief source of Mr. Carnegie's success.

Perhaps there was never anyone associated with Mr. Carnegie who knew him better than did Mr. C. M. Schwab, who, in the following words, has very accurately described that "subtle something" in Mr. Carnegie's personality which enabled him to rise to such stupendous heights:

> I never knew a man with so much imagination, lively
> intelligence, and instinctive comprehension. You sensed
> that he probed your thoughts and took stock of every-

thing that you had ever done or might do. He seemed to catch at your next word before it was spoken. The play of his mind was dazzling and his habit of close observation gave him a store of knowledge about innumerable matters.

But his outstanding quality, from so rich an endowment, was the power to inspire other men. Confidence radiated from him. You might be doubtful about something and discuss the matter with Mr. Carnegie. In a flash he would make you see that it was right and then you would absolutely believe it; or he might settle your doubts by pointing out its weakness. This quality of attracting others, then spurring them on, arose from his own strength.

The results of his leadership were remarkable. Never before in the history of industry, I imagine, was there a man who, without understanding his business in its working details, making no pretense of technical knowledge concerning steel or engineering, was yet able to build up such an enterprise.

In his last sentence, Mr. Schwab corroborates the theory of the Master Mind, to which I attributed Mr. Carnegie's power.

Andrew Carnegie's ability to inspire others rested on something deeper than any faculty of judgment. It is obvious that his success was due to his understanding of his own mind and the minds of other men, and not to mere knowledge of the steel business.

Mr. Carnegie learned how to apply the law of the Master Mind. This enabled him to organize the faculties of his own mind and the faculties of other men's minds, and to coordinate the whole behind a definite chief aim.

Napoleon Hill believed that the law of the Master Mind was his most original and important contribution to Carnegie's philosophy of personal achievement. However, on first reading, many people see nothing more to it than the obvious advantage of cooperation or working together. The editors assure you there is definitely something more to it than that, and the "something more" is directly related to the Law of Attraction.

As you know, the Law of Attraction states that whatever you focus on in your mind acts like a magnet, attracting other like-natured ideas. A Master Mind is formed when two or more people come together to focus on the same thing, and it is the combination of minds that attracts the creative ideas. By definition, the members of a Master Mind are committed to the same philosophy, and with multiple minds focused on the same definite chief aim, all members also have access to a wider, deeper, communal pool of Infinite Intelligence. The combination will produce insights and ideas that the individual minds would never have come up with independently.

The following, adapted from the opening chapter of *Law of Success,* is Hill's explanation of how and why two or more minds coming together can be more than just the sum of the parts.

THE MASTER MIND AND MIND CHEMISTRY

It is my belief that the mind is made up of the same universal energy as that which fills the universe. It is a fact that some minds clash the moment they come in contact with each other, while other minds show a natural affinity for each other.

Some minds are so naturally adapted to each other that love at first sight is the inevitable outcome of the contact. In other cases, minds are so antagonistic that violent mutual dislike shows itself at first meeting. These results occur without a word being spoken, and without the slightest signs of any of the usual causes for love and hate acting as a stimulus.

It is quite probable that the human mind is made up of energy, and when two minds come close enough to form a contact, the mixing of the units of this mind-stuff starts vibrations that affect the two individuals pleasantly or unpleasantly.

Every effect must have a cause. What could be more reasonable than to suspect the cause of the change in attitude between two minds is none other than the disturbance of the electrons of each mind in the process of rearranging themselves in the new field created by the contact?

Every mind has what might be termed an electric field. The nature of this field varies, depending upon the mood of the individual mind and upon the nature of the chemistry of the mind creating the field.

Any individual may voluntarily change the chemistry of his or her mind so that it will attract or repel all with whom it comes in contact. Stated in another way, any person may assume a mental attitude that will attract and please others or repel and antagonize them, and this without the aid of words or facial expression or other form of movement or demeanor.

When two or more people harmonize their minds and produce the effect known as a Master Mind, each person in the group becomes vested with the power to contact and gather knowledge through the subconscious minds of all the other members of the group. This power becomes immediately noticeable in the form of a more vivid imagination and the consciousness of what appears to be a sixth sense. It is through this sixth sense that new ideas will flash into the mind.

If the entire group has met for the purpose of discussing a given subject, ideas concerning that subject will come pouring into the minds of all present, as if an outside influence were dictating them. The minds of those participating in the Master Mind become like magnets, attracting ideas and thoughts of the most highly organized and practical nature.

The following is how Hill explained the same concepts when he wrote *Think and Grow Rich.* This excerpt is adapted from the chapter titled The Power of the Master Mind: The Driving Force.

GAINING POWER THROUGH THE MASTER MIND

Power is essential for success in the accumulation of money. Plans are useless without the power to translate them into action.

Power may be defined as organized and intelligently directed knowledge. Power, as the term is used here, refers to organized effort sufficient to enable an individual to transmute desire into its monetary equivalent. Organized effort is produced through the Master Mind.

The Master Mind may be defined as "coordination of knowledge and effort, in a spirit of harmony, between two or more people, for the attainment of a definite purpose."

No individual may have great power without utilizing the Master Mind. So you may better understand the potential power available to you through a properly chosen Master Mind group, I will explain the two characteristics of the Master Mind principle. One kind of power is economic, and the other psychic.

Economic power: The economic feature is obvious. Economic advantages may be created by any person who surrounds himself with the advice, counsel, and personal cooperation of a group of people who are willing to lend wholehearted aid, in a spirit of perfect harmony.

Psychic power: What I refer to as the psychic phase of the Master Mind principle is a little more difficult to comprehend. You will get a better sense of the meaning from this statement: "No two minds ever come together without creating a third, invisible, intangible force, which may be likened to a third mind." The human mind is a form of energy. When the minds of two people are coordinated in a spirit of harmony, the energy of each mind seems to "pick up on" the energy of the other mind, which constitutes the "psychic" phase of the Master Mind.

HOW TO MULTIPLY YOUR BRAINPOWER

The human brain may be compared to an electric battery. It is a fact that a group of batteries will provide more energy than a single battery. It is also a fact that the amount of energy provided by each individual battery depends upon the number and capacity of the cells it contains.

The brain functions in a similar fashion. Some brains are more efficient than others.

A group of brains coordinated (or connected) in a spirit of harmony will provide more thought-energy than a single brain, just as a group of electric batteries will provide more energy than a single battery.

We return to the excerpt adapted from the opening chapter to *Law of Success*:

The modern radio substantiates, to a considerable extent, this theory. Powerful sending or broadcasting stations must be erected through which the vibration of sound is stepped up before it can be picked up and carried in all directions. A Master Mind made up of many individual minds, so blended that they produce a strong vibrating energy, constitutes almost an exact counterpart of the radio broadcasting station.

Every public speaker has felt the influence of mind chemistry, for it is a well-known fact that as soon as the individual minds of an audience become en rapport with the speaker (attuned to the rate of vibration of the mind of the speaker), there is a noticeable increase of enthusiasm in the speaker's mind, and he often rises to heights of oratory which surprise all, including himself.

It is the same with blending individual minds into a Master Mind. Each mind, through the principle of mind chemistry, stimulates all the other minds in the group, until the mind energy becomes so great that it connects with the universal energy and this, in turn, touches every atom of the entire universe.

Regardless of who you are, or what your definite chief aim may be, if you plan to attain the object of your chief aim through the *cooperative efforts* of others, you must set up in the minds of those whose cooperation you seek a motive strong enough to ensure their full, undivided, unselfish cooperation. When you do, you will be empowering your plans with the law of the Master Mind.

The following is adapted from the chapter titled Cooperation, from *Law of Success*:

It is possible for groups to function cooperatively without creating a Master Mind, such as when people cooperate merely out of necessity and without the spirit of harmony as the basis of their efforts. This sort of cooperation may produce considerable power, but it doesn't compare with what is possible when every person in an alliance subordinates their own individual interests.

The extent to which people may be induced to cooperate, in harmony, depends on the motivating force that impels them to action. The perfect harmony essential for creating a Master Mind develops only when the motivating force of a group is sufficient to cause each member of the group to completely forget his or her own personal interests and work for the good of the group, or for the sake of attaining some idealistic, charitable, or philanthropic objective.

The following is adapted from the chapter titled Organized Planning: The Crystallization of Desire into Action, from *Think and Grow Rich*.

You have learned that everything we create or acquire begins in the form of desire. Desire is taken on the first lap of its journey, from the abstract to the concrete, in the workshop of the imagination, where plans for its transition are created and organized.

There are six definite, practical steps to begin translating your desire for money into its monetary equivalent. One of the steps you must take is the formation of a definite, practical plan, or plans, through which this transformation may be made.

Following are basic instructions for making practical plans:

- Ally yourself with a group of as many people as you may need for the creation and carrying out of your plan or plans for the accumulation of money, making use of the Master Mind principle.

- Before forming your Master Mind alliance, decide what advantages and benefits you may offer the individual members of your group in return for their cooperation. No one will work indefinitely without some form of compensation. No intelligent person should request or expect another to work without adequate compensation, although this may not always be in the form of money.

- Arrange to meet with the members of your Master Mind group at least twice a week, and more often if possible, until you have jointly perfected the necessary plan or plans for the accumulation of money.

- Maintain perfect harmony between yourself and every member of your Master Mind group. If you fail to carry out this instruction to the letter, you may expect to meet with failure. The Master Mind principle cannot work where perfect harmony does not prevail.

WHAT'S IN IT FOR ME?

There are at least three distinctly different advantages that you gain by working with a Master Mind alliance.

1. A Master Mind increases the amount you can do. No matter how intelligent or well-informed you may be, no one person, functioning independently, can ever possess great power. If you try to do it on your own, it will take you longer to do things that others can do faster and better, and in the end you will waste time, money, and energy.

2. A Master Mind improves the quality of what you can do because, in addition to more manpower, it also gives you more knowledge than any single person can have. Through your Master Mind alliance, you combine your advice and knowledge with the advice and knowledge of others who join with you, and the others give you the use of their counsel and contacts just as if they were your own.

3. A Master Mind improves your creativity. When the minds of two or more people are coordinated in a spirit of perfect harmony, when you are working with other people and everyone is on the same wavelength, the energy of each mind seems to pick up on the energy of the other minds. This results in more and better ideas than any one person could ever come up with working alone.

The following is adapted from the chapter titled Concentration, from *Law of Success*:

You will understand from this lesson that the object of forming an alliance between two or more people, and thereby creating a Master Mind alliance, is to apply the law of concentration more effectively than it could be applied through the efforts of one person.

The principle referred to as the Master Mind is nothing more nor less than group concentration of mind power on the attainment of a definite object or end. Greater power comes through group mind concentration because of the "stepping up" process produced through the reaction of one mind on another or others.

Chapter 10

The Law of Attraction

&

The Golden Rule

In reading this book, it is quite likely that at some point you were struck by the thought that there is something very familiar about the Law of Attraction's premise that if you think positively you will manifest positive things in your life, and if you think negatively you will attract negative things to yourself. Turn the words over in your mind a few times and you realize that what it is saying is not that different from the Golden Rule: "Do unto others as you would have them do unto you."

As you will learn in the following pages, Napoleon Hill sees much more than just a similarity in these concepts. In Hill's view they are simply different ways of stating the same basic truth. Although the

Law of Attraction seems focused on your personal desires and what you think to yourself, while the Golden Rule is about what you "do unto others," Hill points out that the way you relate to others is in fact the *physical* manifestation of what you *think* to yourself.

You cannot act in any way toward someone else without first *thinking* about how you are going to act toward that person. Therefore, doing unto others so that they will do the same unto you is a perfect example of your thought transforming itself into reality. The Golden Rule and the Law of Attraction are in fact one and the same.

The following section is excerpted and adapted from the chapter titled The Golden Rule, which appears in *Law of Success*:

The Golden Rule essentially means to do unto others as you would wish them to do unto you—if your positions were reversed.

For more than four thousand years, people have been preaching the Golden Rule as a suitable rule of conduct toward others. But while we have accepted the philosophy of it as a sound rule of ethical conduct, we have failed to understand the spirit of it or the law upon which it is based.

If you fully understood the principles described in earlier chapters—that one's thoughts are transformed into reality corresponding exactly to the nature of the thoughts—it will be quite easy for you to understand the law upon which the Golden Rule is based. You cannot change this law, but you can use it as an irresistible power that will carry you to heights of achievement that could not be attained without its aid.

It is your privilege to deal unjustly with others, but if you understand this law, you must know that your unjust dealings will come home to roost. This law does not stop by merely flinging back upon you your acts of injustice and unkindness toward others; it goes further than this—much further—and returns to you the results of every thought that you release.

Therefore, it is not enough to "do unto others as you wish them to do unto you," but you must also "think of others as you wish them to think of you."

DO UNTO OTHERS . . .

You cannot indulge in an act toward another person without having first created the nature of that act in your own thoughts, and you cannot release a thought without planting the sum and substance and nature of it in your own subconscious mind, where it becomes an integral part of your own character, modifying it in exact conformity with the nature of the act or thought.

Grasp this simple principle and you will understand why you cannot afford to hate or envy another person. You will also understand why you cannot afford to strike back, in kind, at those who do you an injustice. Likewise, you will understand the injunction "return good for evil."

Understand the law upon which the Golden Rule is based and you will also understand the law that eternally binds all mankind in a single bond of fellowship and renders it impossible for you to injure another person, by thought or deed, without injuring yourself. Similarly, the results of every kind thought and deed in which you indulge adds favorably to your own character.

Understand this law and you will then know, beyond room for the slightest doubt, that you are constantly punishing yourself for every wrong you commit and rewarding yourself for every act of constructive conduct.

. . . AS YOU WOULD HAVE THEM DO UNTO YOU

There are people who believe that the Golden Rule philosophy is nothing more than a theory and that it is in no way connected with an immutable law. They have arrived at this conclusion because of personal experience wherein they rendered service to others without enjoying the benefits of direct reciprocation.

How many have not rendered service to others that was neither reciprocated nor appreciated? I am sure that I have had such an experience, not once but many times, and I am equally sure that I will have similar experiences in the future. But I will not discontinue rendering service to others merely because they neither reciprocate nor appreciate my efforts. And here is the reason:

When I render service to another, or indulge in an act of kindness, I store away in my subconscious mind the effect of my efforts, which may be likened to the charging of a battery. By and by, if I indulge in a sufficient number of such acts, I will have developed a positive, dynamic character that will attract people who harmonize with or resemble my own character. Those whom I attract to me will reciprocate the acts of kindness and the service that I have rendered others, thus the law of compensation will have balanced the scales of justice for me, bringing back from one source the results of service that I rendered through an entirely different source.

You can comprehend this law quite easily by regarding yourself as a sort of human magnet that attracts those whose characters harmonize with your own dominating characteristics and repels all who do not so harmonize. Also keep in mind that you are the builder of that magnet, and that you may change its nature so that it will correspond to any ideal to which you may wish to conform.

Again, and most important of all, remember that this entire process of change takes place through thought. Your character is but the sum total of your thoughts and deeds—a truth that has been stated in many different ways throughout this course.

Because of this great truth it is impossible for you to render any useful service or indulge in any act of kindness toward others without benefiting thereby. Moreover, it is just as impossible for you to indulge in any destructive act or thought without paying the penalty in the loss of a corresponding degree of your own power.

Thus, by indulging in acts of kindness and always applying the Golden Rule philosophy, you are sure of benefit from one source and at the same time you have a pretty fair chance of profiting from another source.

It might happen that you would base all your acts toward others on the Golden Rule without enjoying any direct reciprocation for a long period of time. It might also happen that those to whom you rendered those acts of kindness would never reciprocate. In the meantime, however, you have been strengthening your own character, and sooner or later this positive character you have been building will begin to assert itself, and you will discover that you have been receiving compound interest in return for those acts of kindness which appeared to have been wasted on those who neither appreciated nor reciprocated them.

Remember that your reputation is made by others, but your *character* is made by you.

One reason for being just toward others is that such action may cause them to reciprocate in kind, but as I have said, a better reason is that kindness and justice toward others develops positive character in all who do so.

You may withhold from me the reward to which I am entitled for rendering you helpful service, but no one can deprive me of the benefit I will derive from the rendering of that service insofar as it adds to my *own* character.

As Napoleon Hill often notes, the Law of Attraction can work to your benefit or it can work to your detriment. In the following, Hill identifies a variation on the negative aspect that he calls the law of retaliation, which pertains specifically to the Golden Rule and *how* you choose to "do unto others." The following is adapted from the chapter Self-Control, which appears in *Law of Success*.

THE LAW OF RETALIATION

You know what "retaliate" means, but as it is used here it means "to return like for like" and not merely to avenge or to seek revenge, as is commonly meant by the use of this word.

If I do you an injury, you retaliate at first opportunity. If I say unjust things about you, you will retaliate in kind, even in greater measure. On the other hand, if I do you a favor, you will reciprocate in greater measure if possible.

Through the proper use of this law, I can get you to do whatever I wish you to do. If I wish you to dislike me and lend your influence toward damaging me, I can accomplish this by inflicting upon you the sort of treatment that I want you to inflict upon me through retaliation.

If I wish your respect, your friendship, and your cooperation, I can get these by extending to you my friendship and cooperation.

You can compare these statements with your own experience and you will see how beautifully they harmonize.

How often have you heard the remark "What a wonderful personality that person has"? How often have you met people whose personalities you coveted?

The person who attracts you to them through their pleasing personality is merely making use of the law of attraction, or the law of retaliation, both of which, when analyzed, mean that "like attracts like."

The first and probably the most important step to be taken in mastering this law is to cultivate complete self-control. You must learn to take all sorts of punishment and abuse without retaliating in kind. This self-control is a part of the price you must pay for mastery of the law of retaliation.

When an angry person starts in to vilify and abuse you, justly or unjustly, just remember that if you retaliate in a like manner you are being drawn down to that person's mental level, therefore that person is *dominating you!*

On the other hand, if you refuse to become angry, if you retain your self-composure and remain calm and serene, you take the other person by surprise. You retaliate with a weapon with which he is unfamiliar, consequently *you easily dominate him!*

Like attracts like! There's no denying this.

Literally speaking, every person with whom you come in contact is a mental looking glass in which you may see a perfect reflection of your own mental attitude.

Through the principle of retaliation we can actually convert our enemies into loyal friends. If you have an enemy whom you wish to convert into a friend, you can prove the truth of this statement if you will forget that dangerous millstone hanging around your neck, which we call "pride" (stubbornness). Make a habit of speaking to this enemy with unusual cordiality. Go out of your way to favor them in every manner possible. They may seem immovable at first, but gradually he or she will give way to your influence and "retaliate in kind"!

Sometimes it may be necessary to meet force with force, until we overpower our opponent, but while they are down is a splendid time to complete the "retaliation" by taking them by the hand and showing them a better way to settle disputes.

It is for you to decide what you want others to do, and it is for you to get them to do it through the law of retaliation!

In the preceding, Napoleon Hill explained how the law of retaliation turns the concept of "like attracts like" from theory into a practical application. In the following section, Hill explains the way in which another law of nature, which he calls the law of increasing returns, can be used to turn your desire into reality.

This is excerpted and adapted from the chapter titled The Habit of Doing More Than Paid For, taken from *Law of Success*:

THE LAW OF INCREASING RETURNS

Let us begin our analysis by showing how nature employs this law on behalf of the tillers of the soil.

The farmer carefully prepares the ground, then sows his wheat and waits while the law of increasing returns brings back the seed he has sown, plus a manyfold increase.

Were it not for this law of increasing returns, humankind would perish because we could not make the soil produce sufficient food for our existence. There would be no advantage to be gained by sowing a field of wheat if the harvest yield did not return more than was sown.

With this vital "tip" from nature, let us proceed to appropriate this law and learn how to apply it to the service we render, so that it may yield returns in excess of the effort put forth.

Several years ago I was invited to deliver a lecture before the students of the Palmer School in Davenport, Iowa. My manager completed arrangements for me to accept the invitation under the regular terms in effect at that time, which were $100 for the lecture plus my travel expenses.

When I arrived at Davenport I found a reception committee awaiting me at the depot, and that evening I was given one of the warmest welcomes I had ever received during my public career, up to that time. I met many delightful people from whom I gathered many valuable facts that were of benefit to me. Therefore, when I was asked to make out my expense account so the school could give me a check, I told them that I had received my pay, many times over, by what I had learned while I was there. I refused my fee and returned to my office in Chicago feeling well repaid for the trip.

The following morning Dr. Palmer went before the two thousand students of his school and announced what I had said about feeling repaid by what I had learned, and he added: "In the twenty years that I have been conducting this school I have had scores of speakers address the student body, but this is the first time I ever knew a man to refuse his fee because he felt that he had been repaid for his services in other ways. This man is the editor of a national magazine and I advise every one of you to subscribe to that magazine, because such a man as this must have much that each of you will need when you go into the field and offer your services."

By the middle of that week I had received more than $6,000 for subscriptions. During the following two years, these same two thousand students and their friends sent in more than $50,000 for subscriptions. Tell me how or where I could have invested $100 as profitably as this.

I have been thinking for more than twenty-five years about this *privilege* of doing more than paid for, and my thoughts have led me to the conclusion that a single hour devoted each day to rendering service for which we are not paid can be made to yield bigger returns than what we receive from all the rest of the day when we are merely performing our *duty.*

The law of increasing returns is no invention of mine, nor do I lay claim to the discovery of the principle of doing more than paid for as a means of utilizing this law. I merely appropriated them, after many years of observation of those forces that enter into the attainment of success, just as *you* will appropriate them after you understand their significance.

You can begin this process now by trying an experiment that will open your eyes and give you powers that you did not know you possessed.

I am going to ask you to approach this experiment with full faith that it will mark one of the most important turning points of your entire life. I am going to ask you to make the object of this experiment the removal of a mountain that is standing where your success should stand, but where it can never stand until you have removed the mountain.

You may never have noticed the mountain to which I refer, but it is standing there in your way just the same, unless you have already discovered and removed it. And what is this mountain? It is the feeling that you have been cheated unless you receive material pay for all the service you render. That feeling may be unconsciously expressing itself and destroying the very foundation of your success in scores of ways that you have not realized.

In its basic form, this feeling usually seeks outward expression in terms something like, "I am not paid to do this and I'll be damned if I'll do it." You know the attitude to which I refer.

Success must be attracted through understanding and application of laws that are as immutable as is the law of gravity. For this reason, you are requested to enter into the following experiment with the object of further familiarizing yourself with the all-important law of increasing returns.

During the next six months make it your business to render useful service to at least one person every day, for which you neither expect nor accept monetary pay.

Do this experiment with faith that it will reveal one of the most powerful laws of achieving success, and you will not be disappointed.

The rendering of this service may take any form you choose. For example, it may be rendered personally to one or more specific persons. Or it may be rendered to your employer as work that you perform after hours. Or it may be rendered to entire strangers whom you never expect to see again. It doesn't matter to whom you render this service so long as you render it with willingness, and solely for the purpose of benefiting others.

If you carry out this experiment with the proper attitude, you will discover what all others who have become familiar with the law on which it is based have discovered—that you can no more render service without receiving compensation than you can withhold the rendering of it without suffering the loss of reward.

In this lesson we have learned a great principle—probably the most important major principle of psychology! We have learned that our thoughts and actions toward others resemble a magnet which attracts to us the same sort of thought and the same sort of action that we ourselves create.

We have learned that "like attracts like," whether in thought or in action. We have learned that the human mind responds, in kind, to whatever thought impressions it receives. We have learned that the human mind resembles mother earth in that it will reproduce action that corresponds, in kind, to the sensory impressions planted in it. We have learned that kindness begets kindness, and unkindness and injustice beget unkindness and injustice.

We have learned that our actions toward others, whether of kindness or unkindness, justice or injustice, come back to us, in an even larger measure! We have learned that the human mind responds in kind to all sensory impressions it receives; therefore we know what we must do to influence any desired action on the part of another. We have learned that pride and stubbornness must be brushed away before we can make use of the law of retaliation in a constructive way.

Chapter 11

I Am the Captain of My Soul

The following summation presents an overview of many of the ideas and concepts explained in the preceding chapters. This material is excerpted and adapted from the chapter titled Accurate Thinking, in *Law of Success*:

We have discovered that the human body consists of billions of living, intelligent, individual cells that carry on a very definite, well-organized work of building, developing, and maintaining the body.

We have discovered that these cells are directed, in their respective duties, by the subconscious or automatic action of the mind; that the subconscious section of the mind can be, to a very large extent, controlled and directed by the conscious or voluntary section of the mind.

We have found that any idea or thought that is held in the mind, through repetition, has a tendency to direct the physical body to transform such thought or idea into its material equivalent. We have found that any order which is properly given to the subconscious section of the mind, through the law of autosuggestion, will be carried out unless it is sidetracked or countermanded by another and stronger order. We have found that the subconscious mind does not question the source from which it receives orders, nor the soundness of those orders, but it will proceed to direct the body to carry out any order it receives.

This explains the necessity for closely guarding how and from where we receive suggestions. It is a fact that we can be subtly and quietly influenced at times and in ways of which we are not consciously aware.

We have found that every movement of the human body is controlled by either the conscious or the subconscious section of the mind, and that not a muscle can be moved until an order to do so has been sent out by one or the other of these two sections of the mind.

When this principle is thoroughly understood, we also understand the powerful effect of any idea or thought that we create and hold in the conscious mind until the subconscious mind has time to take over that thought and begin the work of transforming it into its material counterpart. When we understand the principle through which any idea is first placed in the conscious mind, and held there until the subconscious picks it up and appropriates it, we have a practical working knowledge of the law of concentration.

THE VALUE OF ADOPTING A CHIEF AIM

This lesson not only describes the real purpose of a definite chief aim, but it also explains in simple terms the principles through which such an aim or purpose may be realized.

First create the objective toward which you are striving, through the imaginative faculty of your mind, then transfer an outline of this objective to paper by writing out a definite statement of it in the nature of a definite chief aim.

By daily reference to this written statement, the idea or thing aimed for is taken up by the conscious mind and handed over to the subconscious mind, which in turn directs the energies of the body to transform the desire into reality.

DESIRE

Strong, deeply rooted desire is the starting point and seed of all achievement. It is the starting place behind which there is nothing, or at least nothing of which we have any knowledge.

A definite chief aim, which is only another name for desire, would be meaningless unless based on a strong desire for the object of that aim. Many people "wish" for many things, but a wish is not the equivalent of a strong desire, and therefore wishes are of little or no value unless crystallized into the more definite form of desire.

It is believed that all energy and matter respond to and are controlled by a law of attraction that causes elements and forces of a similar nature to gather around certain centers of attraction. Likewise, constant, deeply seated desire attracts the physical equivalent or counterpart of the thing desired, or the means of securing it.

SUGGESTION AND AUTOSUGGESTION

Through several lessons of this course, you have learned that sense impressions arising out of one's environment, or from the statements or actions of other people, are called suggestions, while sense impressions that we place in our own minds are placed there by self-suggestion, or autosuggestion.

All suggestions coming from others, or from the environment, influence us only after we have accepted them and passed them on to the subconscious mind through the principle of autosuggestion. Thus it is seen that suggestion must become autosuggestion before it influences the mind of the one receiving it.

Stated another way, no one may influence another without the consent of the one influenced, as the influencing is done through one's own power of autosuggestion.

The conscious mind stands, during the hours when one is awake, as a sentinel, guarding the subconscious mind and warding off all suggestions that try to reach it from the outside until those suggestions have been examined, and accepted, by the conscious mind. This is nature's way of safeguarding the human being against intruders who would otherwise take control of any mind at will.

It is a wise arrangement.

THE VALUE OF AUTOSUGGESTION IN ACHIEVING YOUR DEFINITE CHIEF AIM

One of the greatest uses to which you may direct the power of autosuggestion is in having it help accomplish the object of your definite chief aim in life.

The way to do this is very simple. While the exact formula has been referred to in many other lessons of the course, I will describe again the principle on which it is based.

Write out a clear, concise statement of what you intend to accomplish as your definite chief aim, covering a period of perhaps the next five years. Make at least two copies of your statement, one to be placed where you can read it several times a day while you are at work, and another to be placed where it can be read several times each evening before you go to sleep and just after you arise in the morning.

The suggestive influence of this procedure, impractical though it may seem, will soon impress the object of your definite chief aim on your subconscious mind. Within a very short time you will begin to observe events taking place that will lead you nearer and nearer the attainment of that object.

From the very day that you reach a definite decision in your own mind as to the precise thing, condition, or position in life that you deeply desire, you will observe, if you read books, newspapers, and magazines, that important news items and other data bearing on the object of your definite chief aim will begin to come to your attention. You will also observe opportunities beginning to come to you that will, if embraced, lead you nearer and nearer the coveted goal of your desire.

No one knows better than I how impossible and impractical this may seem to the person who is not a student of psychology. However, the best thing for anyone to do is to experiment with this principle until its practicality has been established.

The word *impossible* means less now than it ever did before in the history of the human race. There are some who have actually removed this word from their vocabularies, believing that we can do anything we can imagine and believe we can do!

We know now that the universe is made up of two substances: matter and energy. Through patient scientific research, we have discovered that everything that is or ever has been in the way of matter, when analyzed to the finest point, is nothing but a form of energy.

On the other hand, every material thing that man has created began in the form of energy, through the seed of an idea that was released through the imaginative faculty of the human mind. In other words, the beginning of every material thing is energy and the ending of it is energy.

All matter obeys the command of one form or another of energy. The highest known form of energy is that which functions as the human mind. The human mind, therefore, is the sole directing force of everything man creates, and what he may create with this force in the future, as compared with what he has created with it in the past, will make his past achievements seem petty and small.

We do not have to wait for future discoveries for evidence that the mind is the greatest force known. We know now that any idea, aim, or purpose that is fixed in the mind and held there, with a will to achieve or attain its physical or material equivalent, puts into motion powers that cannot be conquered.

It seems appropriate to state here that a strong desire, to be transformed into reality, must be backed with persistency until it is taken over by the subconscious mind. It is not enough to feel very deeply the desire for achievement of a definite chief aim, for just a few hours or a few days. The desire must be placed in the mind and held there—with persistence that knows no defeat—until the automatic or subconscious mind takes it over. Up to this point you must stand behind the desire and push it; beyond this point the desire will stand behind you and push you on to achievement.

Persistence may be compared to the dropping of water that finally wears away the hardest stone. When the final chapter of your life has been completed, it will be found that your persistence, or lack of this sterling quality, played an important part in either your success or your failure.

Thoughts

You never can tell what your thoughts will do
In bringing you hate or love,
For thoughts are things, and their airy wings
Are swifter than a carrier dove.
They follow the law of the universe,
Each thing must create its kind,
And they speed o'er the track to bring you back
Whatever went out from your mind.

—ELLA WHEELER WILCOX

Thoughts are things. It is the belief of many that every completed thought starts an unending vibration with which the one who releases it will have to contend at a later time; that man is but the physical reflection of thought that was put into motion by Infinite Intelligence.

All thought is creative. However, not all thought is constructive or positive. If you think thoughts of misery and poverty and see no way to avoid them, then your thoughts will create those very conditions. But reverse the order, and think thoughts of a positive, expectant nature, and your thoughts will create those conditions.

Your thoughts affect your entire personality and attract to you the outward, physical things that harmonize with the nature of your thoughts. This has been made clear in almost every lesson. The reason for this repetition is that nearly all beginners in the study of the mind overlook the importance of this fundamental truth.

When you suggest to your subconscious mind a definite chief aim that embodies a definite desire, you must accompany it with such faith and belief in the realization of that purpose that you can actually see yourself in possession of it. Conduct yourself as you would if you were already in possession of the object of your definite purpose—from the moment you suggest it to your subconscious mind. Enrich it with the full belief that Infinite Intelligence will step in and mature that purpose into reality. Anything short of such belief will bring you disappointment.

Do not question whether the principles of autosuggestion will work. The power to think as you wish to think is the only power over which you have absolute control.

Please consider that last sentence once again—until you grasp its meaning. If it is within your power to control your thoughts, the responsibility then rests upon you as to whether your thoughts will be of the positive or the negative type, which brings to mind one of the world's most famous poems:

Invictus

Out of the night that covers me,
Black as the pit from pole to pole,
I thank whatever gods may be
For my unconquerable soul.

In the fell clutch of circumstance
I have not winced or cried aloud.
Under the bludgeonings of chance
My head is bloody, but unbowed.

Beyond this place of wrath and tears
Looms but the horror of the shade,
And yet the menace of the years
Finds, and shall find, me unafraid.

It matters not how strait the gate,
How charged with punishments the scroll,
I am the master of my fate,
I am the captain of my soul.

—WILLIAM ERNEST HENLEY

You are the "master of your fate" and the "captain of your soul" because you control your own thoughts. And with the aid of your thoughts, you may create whatever you desire.

Highroads Media, Inc. is the publisher of more books and audiobooks by Napoleon Hill than any other publisher in the world. Other titles available:

NEW BOOKS FROM HIGHROADS MEDIA
Napoleon Hill's First Editions (hardcover)
Selling You! (trade paperback)

REVISED & UPDATED EDITIONS
OF *THINK AND GROW RICH*
Think and Grow Rich: The 21st-Century Edition (hardcover)
Law of Success: The 21st-Century Edition (trade paperback)
Think and Grow Rich: The 21st-Century Updated Edition (softcover)
Think and Grow Rich: The 21st-Century Edition Workbook (softcover)

LEATHER-BOUND, GILT-EDGED
COLLECTOR'S EDITIONS
Think and Grow Rich (single volume)
Law of Success (available in four volumes)

THE *THINK AND GROW RICH* SUPERSET
A SPECIALLY BOUND 2-BOOK EDITION
which includes the softcover editions of:
Think and Grow Rich: The 21st-Century Updated Edition
Think and Grow Rich: The 21st-Century Edition Workbook

AUDIOBOOKS AVAILABLE ON CD
Selling You! (abridged audiobook)
Selling You! (unabridged audiobook)
Think and Grow Rich (unabridged and abridged audiobook editions)
Think and Grow Rich: Instant Motivator (original audiobook)
Law of Success (four-volume unabridged audiobook set)
Your Right to Be Rich (unabridged audiobook)
Napoleon Hill's Keys to Success (unabridged and abridged audiobooks)
Believe and Achieve (abridged audiobook)
The Richest Man in Babylon & The Magic Story (original audiobook)
A Lifetime of Riches: The Biography of Napoleon Hill (abridged audiobook)

For more information about Napoleon Hill books and audiobooks, contact:
Highroads Media, Inc., 6 Commerce Way, Arden, NC 28704
telephone: (323) 822-2676
fax: (323) 822-2686
email: highroadsmedia@sbcglobal.net
visit us at our website: www.highroadsmedia.com